THE HEART
of the BIBLE

EXPLORE *the* POWER *of* KEY BIBLE PASSAGES

JOHN
MACARTHUR

NELSON REFERENCE & ELECTRONIC

A Division of Thomas Nelson Publishers

Since 1798

www.thomasnelson.com

The Heart of the Bible

Copyright © 2005 by John MacArthur

Published in Nashville, Tennessee, by Thomas Nelson, Inc.

Published in association with the literary agency of Wolgemuth & Associates, Inc.

Book design and composition by
Kristy Morell, Smyrna, Tennessee

The heart of the Bible/John MacArthur

ISBN 0-7852-5064-6
Indexes included

Printed in the United States of America

1 2 3 4 5 6 7—09 08 07 06 05

CONTENTS

PREFACE

This book grew out of a list of 52 key passages I chose to encourage believers to memorize—one per week for a full year. It was not an easy task to cut my list of favorite passages down to 52. *All* Scripture is given by inspiration of God. *All* Scripture is profitable (2 Timothy 3:16). But these verses are particularly helpful to anyone who wants to get a firm grasp of the truth.

Those who are familiar with my teaching will notice that I have chosen verses that reflect the main themes I have emphasized in my teaching ministry. Those themes encompass the great themes of Scripture. They are the heart of the Bible.

I could have written a very different book. You could make a case that the heart of the Bible is a *story*. There is indeed a narrative that runs from Genesis to Revelation, and its main character is God. The Bible tells how God made the world and human beings (Adam and Eve), how they fell and were judged and received grace, how their descendants fell and were judged and received grace again. It tells how God redeemed and created for Himself a people (Israel) whom He intended to be holy and to be a light to the world, and how they fell and were judged and received grace. It tells how God became flesh among those people in the person of His Son and gave Himself for our salvation—how He died on a cross for our sins and rose from the dead that we might share His life. It tells how God brought the church into being and called people to a new kind of life, and how God's reign will one day be complete.

This book presupposes a knowledge of that story. What this book attempts to do is draw from the great truths that are revealed in that story and join them with the great principles for living that Scripture reveals. It seems to me that for a new believer—or one who desires to be grounded in God's truth—nothing could be more useful than to focus on the nature of the Bible, the nature of God, the nature of salvation, and the nature of discipleship.

I hope that as you read these 52 sections, you will meditate carefully on the Scripture passages rather than on my comments. It is God's Word itself that is perfect and sure and right and pure. His words are able to give life, not mine. As you meditate on them, you will find delight and nourishment and discipline as well. God's promises are a source of comfort, but they are also a sword that cuts into our hearts.

It is my prayer that you will hide God's Word in your heart, that you might not sin against Him—and that you might love Him with all that you are and be transformed into the person He has called you to be. As always, I am thankful to my editors at Thomas Nelson for their help. They suggested that my comments on these passages might be helpful to you in your Christian growth. I hope they are correct about my comments. I know they are right about the usefulness of the heart of the Bible.

John MacArthur

CHAPTER I

THE BIBLE *in* YOUR HEART

THE BIBLE IS NOT JUST A BOOK you read for information. You read it for transformation. The words of Scripture are the very Word of God, and they change your heart as you meditate on them. This is what the Bible claims for itself: it is a perfect treasure that changes us, enlightens us, judges us, equips us, and makes us grow.

As you read the favorite verses I've included in this book, don't just pass over them quickly. Savor them. Repeat them to yourself. Ponder their meaning for your life and allow them to penetrate your heart. That is what Scripture itself tells us to do.

MEDITATING *on the* WORD *of* GOD

> This Book of the Law shall not depart
> from your mouth, but you shall
> meditate in it day and night, that you
> may observe to do according to all that is
> written in it. For then you will make your
> way prosperous, and then you will have
> good success.
>
> —*Joshua 1:8*

Where does the Word of God belong? In your mouth and in your heart. In Joshua 1:8, "this Book of the Law" refers to the five books of Moses, Genesis through Deuteronomy. But the same command can be expanded to refer to all the books of Scripture, the whole Word of God. The command is that it should not depart from your mouth. In other words, it should be a part of your vocabulary all the time. You should be speaking about Scripture and the things Scripture is concerned with at all times.

How can that happen? It will happen when you meditate on it day and night. It's a simple principle. If you saturate your mind and your thoughts with the Word of God it will come out in your speech. If you saturate your mind and thoughts with other things, they will come out in your speech as well. The Book of Proverbs tells us that as a man thinks in his heart, so he is (Proverbs 23:7). Jesus said, "Out of the abundance of the heart, the mouth speaks" (Matthew 12:34). If your heart is full of the Word of God, that's what is going to come out of your mouth. Before that can happen, you have to fill your heart with the Word. That's why meditation is so important.

When you meditate—when you read a verse over and over and contemplate its meaning—it begins to fill your heart. I believe that is why God gave us a book and not a music video. A music video just goes flying by, jumping from one angle to the next, bombarding you with images, and then it's gone. Even the best movie just washes over you like a wave and then recedes. Our experience of it is fleeting. But words on a page are frozen there permanently. You can go back to the same page, the same verse, over and over, and keep meditating on it. You can compare and contrast it to other verses. You can synthesize what several verses say and interpret them carefully. That is meditation—not just a momentary encounter with the truth, but immersion in it. Putting His Word in a book was the best way God could put a tool in our hands that would teach us to meditate.

If you meditate on the Bible day and night, it will start to come out of your mouth. Your speech will be "gracious and seasoned with salt," as Paul says (Colossians 4:6). It will be the kind of talk that edifies, building others up rather than tearing them down (1 Corinthians 14:26; 1 Thessalonians 5:11).

The purpose of meditating on God's commands is "that you may observe to do according to all that is written." The purpose is not just knowledge but obedience. The promise here is that meditation will ultimately produce changed behavior because our hearts will be saturated with the Word of God. David asks in Psalm 19:14, "Let the words of my mouth and the meditation of my heart be acceptable in Your sight, O LORD, my strength and my Redeemer." He is asking, "O LORD, please govern and guard the meditation of my heart." Why? Because that is what is going to show up in my behavior.

As the Bible shapes you as a Christian, it brings blessing. It promises that if you meditate on the Word, speak the Word, and live the Word, your way will be prosperous and you will have good success. This is the real "prosperity gospel"—not the false message that God wants everyone to get rich quick. God does not promise to make you prosperous just because you want things. God promises to bless your spiritual life and your spiritual endeavors with success through the deep understanding and application of Scripture.

DELIGHTING *in the* LAW

Blessed is the man who walks not in the
counsel of the ungodly, nor stands in the

path of sinners, nor sits in the seat of the scornful; but his delight is in the law of the LORD, and in His law he meditates day and night.

—*Psalm 1:1–2*

How can you be blessed? How can you find deep-seated contentment and spiritual well-being below the surface of life's circumstances? These verses are a promise of blessing. They tell us what to avoid and what to focus on.

If you want to be blessed, the psalmist says, don't walk in the counsel of the ungodly. What does that mean? Don't listen to what ungodly people have to say. Don't follow their advice. Don't be influenced by their spin on things, their assessment of the situation, or their solution to a problem.

A three-stage process is pictured here, moving from walking to standing to sitting. It starts with the image of walking alongside ungodly people, engaged in casual conversation. Don't even get started with that, the psalmist says. Don't expose yourself to the lies of people who evaluate the world apart from God's Word.

The next image is standing with the sinners. If you find yourself walking with them, don't allow yourself to stand and talk with them. Don't let the conversation become deeper and more penetrating.

The final image is actually sitting with the scornful—sharing the seat so that you become one of them. Don't get that close to those who mock God. Certainly don't take your seat in their classroom while they scoff at divine truth. Too many young people sit in classrooms where a scornful teacher seeks to destroy their faith.

If you want to be blessed, stay away from all that. Instead, find your delight in the law of the Lord. To most of us today, the idea of delighting in the law is a strange concept. We might fear the law or respect it, but to find pleasure in it is not something that crosses our minds. But the psalmist is thinking of the whole Torah as God's gracious gift of guidance for how to live in a covenant relationship with Him. God's revelation of the right way to live and worship and know Him is something to delight in. Psalm 119 uses the word "delight" eight times to describe our attitude toward God's Word. It is a source of joy and satisfaction.

Rather than delighting in the latest sophisticated way of mocking what is good, find your pleasure in knowing and doing the will of God. Meditate day and night on the Scriptures which reveal His will for your life. Then when you walk, you will walk with the godly; when you stand, you will stand with the righteous; when you sit, you will sit in the place of the holy. This is the path to blessing.

THE DIVERSITY *and* PERFECTION *of* SCRIPTURE

The law of the LORD is perfect,
converting the soul;
The testimony of the LORD is sure,
making wise the simple;
The statutes of the LORD are right,
rejoicing the heart;
The commandment of the LORD is pure,
enlightening the eyes;
The fear of the LORD is clean,
enduring forever;
The judgments of the LORD are true and
righteous altogether.
—*Psalm 19:7–9*

The Bible has more than one function in our lives. The psalmist gives the Scriptures six different titles, reflecting six different facets of a jewel. As "the Law of the Lord," it is God's standard for human conduct. As "the Testimony of the Lord," it is God's self-disclosure, God giving testimony about who He is. As "the Statutes of the Lord," it is the doctrines and principles the Lord wants us to know. As "the Commandment of the Lord," it is the binding and authoritative mandate God gives to us. As "the Fear of the Lord," it is a manual on worship, teaching how to fear and worship God appropriately. As "the Judgments of the Lord," the Scriptures provide for us the verdicts of the divine judge, God Himself. The Bible is all of that.

This psalm also tells us about the character of Scripture. It is perfect. The Hebrew word means complete, comprehensive, covering everything. It is also sure—something reliable, something you can trust to support you. It is also right, directing you down the right path rather than steering you wrong. It is pure. The word actually means clear, translucent, letting light through. It is clean, without stain, without blemish or flaw. Finally, it is true, absolutely true. What a testimony to Scripture: it is perfect, sure, right, pure, clean, and true.

Then the psalmist tells us what the Bible does. It converts the soul, transforming the whole inner person. These are life-changing words. It makes the simple wise. The Hebrew word for "simple" referred to an open door, because simple-minded people were viewed as people who had the doors of their minds wide open. They let everything in—with no discernment—but nothing stayed in. Sometimes I want to say to a person who brags about having an open mind, "Shut it, please. You're letting everything get in and come out. You need to be more discerning than that." The Bible takes the simple-minded, who do not know the difference between what they should value and what is junk, and makes them wise.

The Bible not only brings wisdom; it also brings joy. The Lord's principles for living are the real source of joy for the human heart. It brings light to our eyes, enabling us to see what we could not see, making dark things understandable. It endures forever. We can trust that it doesn't need to be updated for every culture. It is permanently relevant. "The grass withers, the flower fades, but the word of our God stands forever" (Isaiah 40:8). His Word is altogether righteous, producing in us a comprehensive righteousness we could never achieve on our own. What an amazing book! What a reason to praise our God!

DESIRING PURE MILK

> Therefore, laying aside all malice, all deceit, hypocrisy, envy, and all evil speaking, as newborn babes, desire the pure milk of the word, that you may grow thereby.
>
> —*1 Peter 2:1–2*

How do we grow spiritually? The apostle Paul says that we are to grow into maturity, into the full stature of Christ Himself (Ephesians 4:13). How does that happen? It happens, Peter says, when we desire the pure milk of the Word of God the way a newborn baby desires mother's milk.

We have always had babies around the MacArthur house; we have four children and thirteen grandchildren. One thing is very clear about babies—babies want milk. I once held one of my grandsons as a newborn and he had a serious desire for milk. Unfortunately he wanted to nurse and his mother was not there. I was utterly useless to him at that moment. No matter how long he yelled at me, there was nothing I could do for him.

You see, babies basically want milk and nothing else. They don't care what color their clothes are. They don't care what color the crib is. When they're hungry, they don't care about toys or songs or anything else. Just give me the milk! They are absolutely single-minded in their focus.

It is the singularity and simplicity of that desire that is so striking. As the baby grows into a toddler, life gets more complicated. The little child begins to want more than milk, more than food. As you grow older, life gets even more complex and your desires become more diverse.

Peter is saying that if you want to grow spiritually, you need to get back to that simple appetite of a newborn baby and desire just one thing: the pure milk of the Word of God. Set aside everything else. Set aside malice (evil). Set aside anything deceitful. Set aside any hypocrisy, any envy of other people, and speaking evil about other people. Strip yourself of all those things and focus on one thing, feeding yourself on the Bible, wanting that just as badly as a baby wants milk.

It is not only evil that we need to set aside. We need to set aside all the good things that we could be doing that are not the best. We need to set aside all the other things we could be hungry for that will not really help us grow. We need to cultivate an appetite for Scripture. I hope that the favorite verses in this book will help you begin to taste how wonderful God's Word is and create even more hunger for it. Every time you have an opportunity to drink of that pure milk, you should be like a crying baby longing to be satisfied, and drink your fill. That is how you will grow.

THE PURPOSE *of* SCRIPTURE

> All Scripture is given by inspiration of God, and is profitable for doctrine, for reproof, for correction, for instruction in righteousness, that the man of God may be complete, thoroughly equipped for every good work.
>
> *—2 Timothy 3:16–17*

These verses, taken together as one sentence, tell us not only *how* Scripture was given—by divine inspiration—but also *why* Scripture was given. For what purpose did God give us the Bible? We can understand the answer by starting at the end of the sentence and working our way backwards.

The goal is that we will do good works. These are not good works we do in order to be saved. These are not works that merely seem good in our own eyes. They are works that are truly good according to God's standards and bring honor to Him. Jesus said, "Let your light so shine before men, that they may see your good works and glorify your Father in heaven" (Matthew 5:16). Equipping us to do the things that bring glory to God is the purpose of Scripture.

To be equipped to do that, we have to be "complete." The word here means mature, grown up, and capable. How do we get to that kind of maturity? It requires a process by which we are equipped and made mature, and it includes four things: doctrine, reproof, correction, and instruction in righteousness.

It all starts with doctrine. What does doctrine mean? Teaching! We have to be taught the content of the Bible, but it has to be the kind of teaching that works on us. How does it work on us? First, it reproves us. We need teaching that confronts our sin and confronts our wrong thinking. It points out where the errors lie. Then we need teaching that corrects the errors. Reproof points to a crooked place in our thinking, while correction straightens it out. We need teaching that does both—first breaking down, exposing what is wrong, and then restoring, bringing us back to right. Finally, we need teaching that instructs us how to walk in that righteous path.

Where are we going to find truth that eliminates error, brings correct belief, and sets us on the right path? This passage says "All Scripture." All Scripture is profitable for those things. The Bible is profitable—useful to us—because it brings sound teaching that tears down what is wrong and builds up what is right. It puts us on the path of living so that we can become mature and equipped to do the works that honor God. All Scripture does this.

It does this because it is given by inspiration of God. The Greek word is "God-breathed." Scripture comes out of the mouth of God, and when you read the Bible you are reading the very Word of God. Men wrote it down, but God breathed it out. It is that powerful, living Word of God that brings us the truth and equips us for every good work.

THE WORD *that* CUTS

> For the word of God is living and powerful, and sharper than any two-edged sword, piercing even to the division of soul and spirit, and of joints and marrow, and is a discerner of the thoughts and intents of the heart.
>
> —*Hebrews 4:12*

Do you think of the Bible as a nice book? Many people think of it as a book of religious stories. Christians often think of the Bible as a comforting book, an encouraging book, a book that builds you up. But the Bible itself claims to be a sword—alive, powerful, and sharp. It cuts like the knife of a surgeon, all the way down into the depths of your soul and spirit, cutting into your joints and into the marrow of your bones. That is vivid imagery. It sounds like something that hurts. The Bible is not just a lotion we rub on to soothe us; it is a blade that penetrates deep into us. It knows our thoughts and intentions better than we do.

Nothing cuts and penetrates like the truth of God. All the psychology and philosophy in the world cannot invade you to the depths of your soul like the Word of God can. No psychologist or philosopher could ever know you the way God knows you. Jesus said (John 2:25) that He did not need anyone to tell Him what was in the heart of man because He already knew what was there. Your heart is completely exposed to God. He sees right into you. His insight penetrates into your soul.

Nobody knows you like God. No book gets to the core of your heart the way the Bible does, in both a negative and positive way. When we are down, the Bible knows how to pick us up and comfort us or build us up. But when we are up— elevated by pride or human wisdom—the Bible knows how to bring us down by uncovering our sin, unmasking our hypocrisy, and demolishing our willfulness.

Reading the Bible is not a safe thing to do. It can be a frightening experience. But wherever God cuts with His Word, He heals. Whatever He reveals, He exposes for the sake of cleansing. Jesus said (John 15:2) that we are like branches on a vine that the gardener prunes. We have to be pruned or cut so that we can bear fruit. It is the Word that does that cutting.

I am grateful for the Word of God as a source of comfort, hope, joy, worship, and praise. I am also grateful for the Word of God as a penetrating, convicting, discerning sword that doesn't let me get away with anything. As I expose my life to the Word of God, my sin is revealed. When sin is revealed it can be dealt with. It is that kind of cleansing that makes me able to bear more fruit, to my own joy and to the glory of God.

CHAPTER 2

KNOWING *and* TRUSTING
OUR GREAT GOD

SOMETIMES THE GOD we encounter in the Bible and in creation seems so expansive and complex that we wonder if we are capable of knowing Him at all. He is the God who set the stars in the heavens and shaped human history by His mighty acts. At other times the God of our Christian experience is so intimate and familiar that we lose sight of His greatness. He is our heavenly Father who knows our every need, to whom we can take every sorrow.

The Scripture reveals that God is so great that we can never understand Him completely, but He wants to be known by us. He created us for a relationship with Himself, and He placed within us a desire to know Him. God also wants us to trust in Him, even beyond the limits of our knowing.

LONGING *for* GOD

O GOD, You are my God;
Early will I seek You;
My soul thirsts for You;
My flesh longs for You
In a dry and thirsty land
Where there is no water.
So I have looked for You in the sanctuary,
To see Your power and Your glory.
Because Your lovingkindness is better
    than life,
My lips shall praise You.

—Psalm 63:1–3

This prayer is all about longing. The psalmist rises early in the morning and he is thirsty, but he is not thirsty for water. He is thirsty for God, who is the first thing he wants in the morning. In his spiritual life he is like a wanderer in the desert yearning for a drink. In fact, David was in the desert when he wrote this psalm, hiding out but longing to be back in Jerusalem where he could worship. He was like the deer in the desert hills of Psalm 42:1, "As the deer pants for the water brooks, so pants my soul for You, O God."

This is the heart of a true believer. This is the panting heart, the thirsty heart, the hungry heart that can be satisfied only by the presence and the power of God. What did he want to see? He wanted to see God's power manifested in his life, God's glory revealed in worship. He wanted to experience God's lovingkindness—God's mercy and grace—so that he could offer praise. This was the priority in David's life.

What do you long for in life? What do you yearn for in the blank stretches of the night and when you first rise in the morning? Is it someone to love, or some measure of success, or a new car or home? Right now, if you were to write down the three things you most desire, would knowing and experiencing God be at the top of the list? The apostle Paul could say "All I want is to know Christ" (Philippians 3:10 GNB). His prayer for the Ephesians was that they might grow in the knowledge of God (Ephesians 1:17). Is that what you want for yourself?

Let this be your prayer: *Oh God, it's You I want. I want You in my life. I feel dry and thirsty. I feel weak and lonely. I need Your power, Your glory, Your lovingkindness. It means more to me than life itself, and I want to praise You.*

Boasting *about* Knowing God

Thus says the Lord: "Let not the wise man glory in his wisdom, let not the mighty man glory in his might, nor let the rich man glory in his riches; but let him who glories glory in this, that he understands and knows Me, that I am the Lord, exercising lovingkindness, judgment, and righteousness in the earth. For in these I delight," says the LORD.

—*Jeremiah 9:23–24*

What is it that you glory in? To "glory" in something means to boast about it. What do you boast about?

We live in a world full of people who glory in their wisdom. They put a long string of degrees after their names. They want people to be impressed by their academic achievements, by how smart they are. The world is full of people who glory in their strength. Professional athletes today are constantly boasting about their own physical strength and skill. Business people boast about the strength of their leadership and entrepreneurial ability. And the world is certainly full of people who glory in their riches. They want everyone to know they are wealthy. They wear their riches on their bodies as expensive clothing and jewelry. They drive around in their riches in the form of a luxury car. They live in a house that says "riches" to everyone who passes by. That is the way fallen human beings are: we glory in our own wisdom, strength, and wealth.

But the prophet Jeremiah says that this is what the Lord says: "If you're going to boast, boast about this: that you know me and understand me." That's what we have to boast about as Christians. Paul says

(1 Corinthians 1:26–29) that there are not many Christians who are among the noble or powerful in this world. God chose the lowly and humble and weak. We can't say that we are the wisest people in the world. We can't say that we are the strongest people in the world. But we can say this: we know and understand God.

I was sitting in the middle seat on a low-cost airliner next to a man who looked Middle Eastern when he noticed that I was reading a Bible. He said, "Could I ask you a question?"

"Sure," I replied.

He said, "I'm new in America. I immigrated from Iran and I'm confused about American religion. Everybody in my country is Muslim, but there are so many religions here. Can you tell me about American religion?"

"Sure, what's your question?"

He asked, "What is the difference between a Catholic, a Protestant, and a Baptist?"

I explained the differences to him in a simple way, and then I said, "Can I ask you a question?"

"Of course," he said.

I asked, "Are you a sinner?"

"Oh, yes," he answered. "I sin."

I said, "Well, in your faith, what happens to sinners?"

"Oh, they could go to hell."

I asked him, "Do you have any hope that *you* might not go to hell?"

He said, "I hope that God will forgive me."

I said to him, "Well, I know God and He won't." The man was stunned.

He looked at me and said, "You know God?" I could imagine him thinking, *What are you doing in the middle seat on a bargain airline if you know God? Don't you have any more pull than that?*

It was not easy to tell him that I know God, but I needed to tell him about the God I know. I told him about the God described in Jeremiah 9:24. He is a God who exercises lovingkindness toward all people, including Iranians. But he is also a God who exercises judgment and righteousness in the world. Those who do not know Him—those who have not come to know Him through His Son—will be under God's judgment and will be in hell. But the good news is that people of every nation can be forgiven by trusting in Christ.

I know God. It's amazing but true that a small, finite creature like me can know the God of the universe. God has made Himself known to me in Jesus Christ and in His Word. Why would I want to glory in human wisdom or human might or human riches, when I can glory in the reality that I know the God of the universe? The relationship that I have with God is more precious than intelligence or strength or wealth.

My knowledge of God is precious to me, but even more am I precious to God. That is the wonderful truth at the end of verse 24: God delights in those who understand and know Him. If you know God as He has revealed Himself in the Bible, if you understand that He is a God who exercises both love and judgment, God delights in you.

TRUSTING *in the* LORD

Trust in the LORD with all your heart,
And lean not on your own understanding;
In all your ways acknowledge Him,
And He shall direct your paths.
—*Proverbs 3:5–6*

This command really gets to the core of our Christian living. Do you trust the Lord completely? "With all your heart" means that you trust Him with everything, with all that you are. Can you trust the Lord no matter what comes, good or bad? Can you trust Him no matter what pain or suffering you have to endure, no matter what trial you have to face? Will you trust Him when your dreams crash and burn? Do you trust the Lord wholeheartedly, no matter what?

The alternative is to trust yourself, to lean on your own understanding. We can choose to trust our own interpretation of events instead of trusting that God is directing our paths. When things in your life seem out of control, you have to remember that God loves you and that in all things He is working for your good. We're not meant to understand everything that happens to us. We are meant to learn to trust God rather than trusting our own ability to make sense of things.

One of my favorite books in the Bible is the Book of Job. He had more problems than most of us can imagine. All of his children were killed when they were worshiping God in one of his son's homes. Then he lost all his animals, all his crops, all his wealth. Then he became sick and sat in ashes mourning and scraping boils off his body. The only thing he had left was his wife, and she was no help. She told him to curse God and die.

Job had some friends who came over, and for the first week they just hung around and did not say anything. They just cried with Job and patted him on the back. That was wise and good. But after seven days the friends opened their mouths and all their wisdom disappeared. They reached ridiculous conclusions about his predicament and blamed it all on Job's sin. They thought they were being very spiritual and helpful. They had their own understanding of events, and it was dead wrong.

Finally Job himself asked the Lord, "How am I going to understand this? My heart is right. I'm a man of integrity. I can't find any sin in my life. I have no idea why all this has happened to me." Job did not know that God was allowing Satan to test his faith to prove that saving faith cannot be broken by tragedy. Job asked God to explain to him why he was suffering. God's answer was, "No, I'm not going to explain it to you. Why should I explain anything to you? What makes you think you could understand?" God revealed to Job His creative power and His infinite greatness.

At the end Job simply said, "I have heard of You by the hearing of the ear, but now my eye sees You. Therefore I . . . repent in dust and ashes" (Job 42:5–6). He was saying, in effect, I'm sorry I ever questioned you. I'm just going to trust you. In response to that trust, God gave Job back another family and greater blessings than he had known before.

You cannot lean on your own interpretation of the things that happen in your life. You can only lean on the Lord. Trust Him wholeheartedly. In everything acknowledge Him. He will open up a path that you never even expected. This is His promise.

THE GOD WHO KEEPS US

> Now to Him who is able to keep you from stumbling, and to present you faultless before the presence of His glory with exceeding joy, to God our Savior, Who alone is wise, be glory and majesty, dominion and power, both now and forever. Amen.
>
> —*Jude 24–25*

These verses are what we call a doxology, an expression of praise to God. There are many such doxologies scattered through the Old and New Testaments. This one is often used as a benediction at the close of Christian worship, just as it closes the Letter of Jude. It is a blessing pronounced on God for His greatness, but at the same time it pronounces a blessing on you, because it reminds you that God is able to keep you from stumbling and present you faultless before the presence of His glory with exceeding joy.

What does that mean? It means that God is not going to lose you. He is not going to let go of you. You are never going to fall from His grace. God will keep you from stumbling, from falling into the temptation of abandoning the faith and denying Christ. In the end, He will present you to Himself faultless.

How can that be, when you are not faultless now? When that day comes, when you enter into the presence of God's glory in heaven, it will be a new you that God presents to Himself. Your fallen human nature will have disappeared. You will have been changed into the likeness of Christ. You will never be perfect in this life, but on that day you will be made perfect and holy, without blemish or fault. No wonder there will be exceeding joy!

This is God's promise: if you are Christ's, He will keep you. Jesus said, "All that the Father gives Me will come to Me, and the one who comes to Me I will by no means cast out" (John 6:37). He said, "Of those whom You gave Me I have lost none" (John 18:9). "This is the will of Him who sent Me, that everyone who sees the Son and believes in Him may have everlasting life; and I will raise him up at the last day" (John 6:40).

Everyone the Father gives to Christ, Christ receives. Everyone He receives, He keeps. Everyone He keeps, He raises to eternal glory.

So we can praise our God for keeping His promises and for keeping us. God is our Savior. He alone is wise. To Him alone belong all glory and majesty, all dominion and power, now and forever. Amen.

CHAPTER 3

UNDERSTANDING GOD'S REIGN

I᙭ IS ONE THING TO UNDERSTAND that God reigns over the whole world, and another thing entirely to understand that God controls the circumstances of your life and the trials you face. The sovereignty of God is not an abstract doctrine reserved for theologians. It is a biblical concept that affects the way you view every day of your life.

Why does God let bad things happen to us? Why would He allow us to be tempted? Am I in a tug of war between God and Satan? If God does control the circumstances, do I really have free will? These are some of the questions we'll think about in this chapter as we consider some tremendously powerful verses.

GOD CAUSES ALL THINGS *to* WORK *for* GOOD

> And we know that all things work together for good to those who love God, to those who are the called according to His purpose.
>
> —*Romans 8:28*

Is everything that happens to you good? That is not what this verse is saying. It says that God works even bad things together for the good of those who love God.

Christians don't deny that there is plenty of evil in the world. Christians don't even deny that there is plenty of evil in *them*. No doubt you can relate to Paul's confession in Romans 7:19: "I find myself doing what I don't want to do, and I find myself not doing what I want to do." He cries out, "O wretched man that I am!" (7:24) and confesses, "In my flesh there is nothing good" (7:18). So Romans 8:28 is not saying that there is nothing bad. It says that even what is bad in us can be worked together for good.

Notice that the verse does not say that things work themselves together for good all by themselves. That is what the world thinks: that "things will work out." But the best Greek manuscripts of this verse make it clear that the subject of the sentence is not *things* but *God*. "We know that God causes all things to work together for good" (NASB).

This points us to an immensely important element of God's character. We could call it the *sovereignty* of God. That is His supreme authority and power over all the issues of life, to produce out of them His own good purposes. We could also call it the *providence* of God. That is the wonderful way in which God takes all the vicissitudes of life—all the contingencies, all the choices, all things good, bad, and indifferent—and weaves them all together for a good purpose.

This promise is not for everyone. God does not say that everything will work out OK for everyone in the world. This is a promise made only for those who love God, those who have been called to salvation. If you are a believer, then you can be sure that it was God's purpose to call you to salvation. Not everything in your life will be good, but everything in your life will work together because of God's sovereign providence.

You might not see this at the time, but every suffering, every temptation, every trial, even every sin, God weaves together into a tapestry that is ultimately for your good. Sometimes looking at your situation is like looking at the back of an oriental rug. All you can see is a bunch of threads going in every direction. It appears chaotic. But if you turn the rug over, you see a beautiful pattern. When your life is turned over someday in eternity, you will see the pattern. You will see how God worked it all together for good.

Even in our trials and temptations, God is working for good. Did it surprise you when I said that God even works our *sins* together for good? When I see sin in my life, I resent it and hate it, so the sin itself increases my longing for holiness. Even as I stumble through my life, God uses that stumbling to increase my distaste for sin. Concerning the life to come, God is working all the issues of our present life to produce an eternal reward which we will enjoy forever in His presence.

Do not expect everything in life to be good. It will not happen. Do not expect everything in yourself to be good. That will not happen, either. But what you can expect is this: God will weave everything together for His own beloved children to produce a good result, both in time and for all eternity.

GOD LIMITS OUR TEMPTATIONS

> No temptation has overtaken you except such as is common to man; but God is faithful, who will not allow you to be tempted beyond what you are able, but with the temptation will also make the way of escape, that you may be able to bear it.
>
> —*1 Corinthians 10:13*

Temptation is part of being human. The Scripture says it is common to everyone. I've heard preachers blame every temptation on demons. People claim to be attacked by the demon of anger or the demon of lust—or even the demon of post-nasal drip! But temptation is not really about demons. Temptation is just about being human.

You don't need to go through life in horror and dread of some demonic invasion, as if a superhuman power is going to come and take over your will. If you are a Christian, you are God's and Christ's. "He who is in you is greater than he who is in the world" (1 John 4:4). God is greater than the Evil One. If you are God's child, the only temptations you will ever experience are those that are human. God is never going to let you face a temptation that is beyond your ability to resist.

We face different temptations at different stages in our Christian life. Some things that are very difficult for a brand new baby Christian just coming out of the world are really not a problem to a mature believer who has walked with the Lord for decades. The mature believer still faces temptations, but they are of a different kind, more subtle and harder to recognize. But the Lord guards us at each stage of our journey. He permits us to be tempted only in ways we are able to deal with at the time.

That truth is illustrated by the way Jesus protected His disciples when the Roman soldiers came to take Him captive. The soldiers entered the garden and approached Jesus, and He asked, "Whom are you seeking?" They answered, "Jesus of

Nazareth." He asked them again, "Whom are you seeking?" Again they answered, "Jesus of Nazareth." Then He said, "I AM," and they all fell down.

Why did Jesus ask the soldiers to articulate whom they had come for? He wanted them to personally acknowledge that they had no right to arrest the disciples. He said, "If you are looking for me, let these others go." He knew that if the disciples had been taken captive that night by the Romans, their faith was so weak that they would have abandoned their faith. So Jesus made sure that they were never put in that position. They were protected from facing a temptation they would not have been able to bear. John 18:9 says that Jesus did this to fulfill the Scripture, "Of those whom You gave Me I have lost none."

God is not going to lose you, either. He is personally involved in your life, sheltering you from any temptation that would overwhelm you. We sometimes think God only cares for us in a very general way, dictating that things will happen in a certain way and then letting them happen. But God is much more intimately engaged in our lives than that, protecting us every moment. You will face temptations. But they will never be more than human and they will never be more than you can bear. There will always be a way of escape, so that you can bear it. Often that way of escape will become clear to you in the midst of the temptation. Often the way of escape is simply the path of resistance, the path of obedience, and the path of prayer for God's help.

Trials Make Us Grow Up

> My brethren, count it all joy when you fall into various trials, knowing that the testing of your faith produces patience. But let patience have its perfect work, that you may be perfect and complete, lacking nothing.
>
> —James 1:2–4

This passage gives us another way to think about the temptations we face. The word translated "trials" here is the same word translated "temptations" in 1 Corinthians 10:13 (above). Not only does God protect us from temptations we cannot bear; He also uses those temptations to help us to mature.

We would all love to be able to say that we lack nothing—that we are perfect and complete. We would like the Lord to say that we have nothing missing in our lives. But we can arrive at that state only through pain. We cannot be mature without developing patience, and we cannot develop patience without passing through difficult experiences that test our faith. That is why James says you should count it all joy when you fall into various trials–when you face temptations and tests of your faith. You are being strengthened in those trials by the development of spiritual endurance.

If you want to get stronger physically, what do you do? You put yourself through painful experiences. You go to the gym and work and work, whether it's lifting weights or running the treadmill or spending time on the Stepmaster. You do everything you can to strengthen your body, and you know that there will be pain involved, but you determine that the goal is worth the pain. In order to get strong, you have to be able to endure some pain and persevere in spite of it. It is easy to start, but hard to stay with it.

The same is true if you want to get stronger spiritually. You are never going to become spiritually mature unless you develop endurance, and you can only develop endurance as you persevere in faith through painful experiences. Some people pray, "Lord, I want to be strong for you. I want to be bold and courageous. I want to be grown-up, fully mature, complete in my faith." If you pray that way, brace yourself, because the answer to that prayer is going to be painful. The only way God can answer that prayer is to test your faith by taking you to the edge, pushing you beyond your comfort zone and carrying you through hard times.

If you want that for your life—if you want to be all that God wants you to be for His glory—then you won't just grit your teeth and endure the trial.

You will count it all joy, as James says. How can you do that? You look past the trial, past the pain, to its effect. You look to the purpose of that time of testing in your life, the goal of spiritual maturity. That is where the joy comes from. As you become stronger, you will be less likely to give in to temptation and less likely to waver in your faith. Don't you want that for yourself? If you do, welcome those trials that will make you strong.

WE DIE *with* CHRIST *but* LIVE *by* FAITH

> I have been crucified with Christ; it is no longer I who live, but Christ lives in me; and the life which I now live in the flesh I live by faith in the Son of God, who loved me and gave Himself for me.
>
> —*Galatians 2:20*

This is a wonderful statement of a Christian's own spiritual identity. Paul starts with this fact: "I was crucified with Christ." That looks back to the historical event of the Cross when we were one with Christ as He bore our sins. Were you there when they crucified my Lord? Yes, you were. All of us who believe in Jesus Christ were there at the Cross. God placed us there even though we hadn't been born. Everyone who ever believed—whether the Old Testament saints looking forward to the Messiah, or His followers in the New Testament, and every believer since—all of us who have been forgiven were there in Christ at His death. We shared His death. Paul says in Romans 6 that we were buried with Him and were raised with Him to newness of life. What an incredible reality! Our sins were paid for because we were crucified with Christ. That is why we are not under any condemnation. That's why Jesus said just before He died, "It is finished" (John 19:30). The penalty was paid in full. The list of charges against us was wiped out. God wrote "cancelled" over our debt.

Now we live a new life, raised with Christ in oneness with Him. Paul says it is not really I who live; it is Christ who is living in me. This is a profound mystery, because clearly Paul is still alive. He says that he is living his life in the flesh by faith in the Son of God. Which is it? Am I the one living in my body or is it Christ?

This is one of those paradoxes of the Christian faith that people often ask me to explain. They say, "John, can you explain the sovereignty of God and human choice? Can you explain election and free will?" No, I can't. I can just tell you they are both in the Bible. I don't understand how God harmonizes in His mind that if I'm saved, it is by God's doing, but if I reject Him, it is my doing. That is beyond my grasp, which makes me more confident that men did not write the Bible: Human editors and writers would have fixed things like that to make it seem more logical, but God presented them in such a way as to leave us wondering at how His wisdom is beyond ours.

If I asked you who wrote Galatians, what would you say? Was it Paul or the Holy Spirit? It was all Paul, and it was all the Holy Spirit. How can that be? If I asked you whether Jesus was God or man, what would you say? You know he was 100 percent God and 100 percent man. How can you be 200 percent? It is beyond our understanding.

So if I ask you who lives your Christian life, what will you say? You might say, "I do. I bring my body into subjection. I obey the Word of God." You would be right. But you might also say, "I have to let go and let God. I have to let Christ live his life through me. The Holy Spirit flows through me." You would also be right. In every major doctrine that relates to the saving work of God, there are two truths that have to be held together. We cannot harmonize everything. We just state the two truths and affirm them both.

Paul tells us that this is the great mystery of the Christian life. I have been crucified with Christ. I no longer live. Christ lives in me. But at the same time, I live right now in this fleshly body by faith in Him. It takes all of us, but it is all of Him. It takes all the discipline, obedience, and faith we can muster to live the Christian life, and yet when it is all said and done it is Christ Himself who is living in me, the One who loved me.

CHRIST HAS OVERCOME *the* WORLD

> These things I have spoken to you, that in
> Me you may have peace. In the world you
> will have tribulation; but be of good
> cheer, I have overcome the world.
>
> —*John 16:33*

Jesus said these words in the Upper Room on the night He was betrayed. It was the conclusion of the long farewell speech that begins, "Let not your hearts be troubled" (John 41:1). Jesus told His disciples that He was going away. He told them that they would be worried and fearful, that they would be persecuted, that they would be scattered and abandon Jesus. But all through the speech He made promises that He would not abandon them. His love would continue. He would give the Holy Spirit to encourage them as Jesus had. He promised to answer their prayers.

At the end of the speech, He said, "The purpose of everything I've said to you tonight is that you might have peace in your hearts. You have nothing to be anxious about. I do not mean that you will have no trouble. I have already warned you about persecution. In this world you *will* have trouble." The Greek word has a root meaning of "pressure." You will be under pressure, squeezed by the troubles of this life. But in the midst of that, be of good cheer. That expression sounds vaguely British, doesn't it? "Be of good cheer, old chap!" It means be

THE HEART OF THE BIBLE

happy, be encouraged, take heart—because in the end, I have overcome the world.

The battle has already been decided, Jesus says. There is nothing the world can do to you that can defeat you ultimately, because I have won an absolute victory over sin and death. I am about to finish that work on the Cross. The world—the forces that oppose God—will continue to give you trouble, but they cannot defeat you because I have already won. Their attacks against you can do no real harm because the whole world system opposed to God has been smashed. I have overcome the world. While you remain in that world, you will have trouble. But while you remain in Me, you will have peace.

CHAPTER 4

WHAT HAPPENED *on the* CROSS

AT THE HEART OF THE CHRISTIAN FAITH lies an event. It was a real event in history, a unique one which cannot be repeated. It was the death of the Son of God on the Cross.

The Cross lies at the center of the message of the New Testament. Most Americans know the basic story of how Jesus died. The recent movie, *The Passion of the Christ,* retold that story in a dramatic if violent way that left millions of people stirred by the depth of Jesus' suffering. Many people know that Jesus died, but they do not understand *why* He died.

Theologians have written long treatises on what God did on the Cross—what they call *theories of atonement.* You don't need elaborate theories to understand what the Cross means to you. A few key verses will make the matter clear enough.

> Surely He has borne our griefs and carried our sorrows; yet we esteemed Him stricken, smitten by God, and afflicted. But He was wounded for our transgressions, He was bruised for our iniquities; the chastisement for our peace was upon Him, and by His stripes we are healed. All we like sheep have gone astray; we have turned, every one, to his own way; and the LORD has laid on Him the iniquity of us all.
>
> —*Isaiah 53:4–6*

On the cross Jesus was not suffering for His own sins. He bore the grief for *our* sin. He carried the sorrow for *our* lawlessness. He was wounded for *our* transgressions. He was bruised for *our* iniquities. The prophet Isaiah made that clear centuries before Jesus died.

Who killed Jesus? People continue to debate whether the Jews or the Romans were more responsible. Others say that we are all responsible, since He died for our sins. But Isaiah says something shocking—that Jesus was stricken, smitten, and afflicted by *God*. It was God who placed all our sins on Jesus.

Why God? Because God is the judge of the whole world. He alone has the wisdom to determine the appropriate punishment for our sin, and God gave that punishment to His Son. God was literally the executioner of His own Son. This does not mean that God is a cruel, sadistic Father; it means that He is a compassionate, merciful Father who did the only thing He could to forgive us of our sin. No other sacrifice would have been sufficient for the sin of the whole world. No other sacrifice would have been morally perfect, a spotless Lamb. For God to carry out His righteous judgment on our sin and still forgive us, God became a perfect human sacrifice. The Father sent His only Son to die in our place.

The only way for us to have peace with God was for Jesus to be chastised, punished by God even though He was innocent. By His stripes—those wounds caused by whipping—we are healed spiritually. Because He suffered, we were made right with God. Isaiah says that we all needed to be made right with God. All of us were like wandering sheep who had gone astray. Every one of us had followed his own sinful path, but the Lord gathered up all of the iniquity in all of us and laid it on Jesus Christ. That is the amazing reality of what Jesus Christ, God's Son, did as a substitute for sinners. The sinless One offered Himself for the sinful ones. Every one of us has sinned, but every one of us who trusts in Jesus Christ has that sin paid for.

When we put our trust in Christ, His death is applied to us. Our sins are covered forever and His righteousness is given to us as a gift. This great truth causes us to rejoice supremely, because what God did on the Cross rescues us from eternal judgment and gives us eternal peace with God.

Dying *for the* Ungodly

> For when we were still without strength, in due time Christ died for the ungodly. For scarcely for a righteous man will one die; yet perhaps for a good man someone would even dare to die. But God demonstrates His own love toward us, in that while we were still sinners, Christ died for us.
>
> —*Romans 5:6–8*

Paul focuses our attention on one powerful truth: Christ did not die for us because we were godly. He did not die for the religious or the moral or the good. He died for us, the ungodly, while we were still sinners.

It's rare enough that people die for other people. Occasionally we read about someone giving up his life in a war or a disaster to save another person. Paul acknowledges that in a rare instance someone might die for a righteous person, someone who deserved to be saved. It would be a remarkable person who gave up his life to save a good person. But have you ever heard of anyone willing to die for someone evil? Would anyone die for a man who was wretched, wicked, and vile? Only Jesus Christ would.

This is what real love is—the kind of love the Bible tells us about. It is the kind of love that caused Christ to die for the worst, not the best. That's the wonder of God's love. His amazing love toward us is demonstrated by the fact that Christ died for us while we were still sinners. God's love had nothing to do with our attractiveness or worthiness. It had only to do with God's nature—the fact that God *is* love.

Christ did not die for us because we were so worthy or so loveable or so godly. Paul says that we were without strength, helpless, and unable to save ourselves. There was nothing in us to admire, but God loved us. Christ died for us *because* we were unworthy and helpless. You can't put the gospel any more directly than that: Christ died for the ungodly, not the righteous. He did it because of His own love for us—not for any other reason. A love we did not deserve produced a sacrifice we did not deserve. But that is what grace does.

That love, that sacrifice, produces gratitude in our lives. I hope you are overwhelmed with gratitude every day, never forgetting how unworthy you are of the love of God in Jesus Christ. We have done nothing to deserve His mercy. We have no desirable attributes to attract His love. Even though we were helpless and godless, even when we were in rebellion against Him, God showed His love for us by sending Christ to die instead of us.

Becoming Sin *for* Us

> For He made Him who knew no sin to be
> sin for us, that we might become the
> righteousness of God in Him.
> —*2 Corinthians 5:21*

This verse has only fifteen words in the original Greek, but those fifteen words express the doctrine of substitution like no other verse in the Bible. That idea of substitution lies at the heart of the gospel. Who was it who knew no sin? There was only one person who ever lived without sin, and that was Jesus Christ. God made Jesus, who never sinned, to be sin for us.

What does it mean that God made Christ to be sin? Some people teach that Jesus actually became a sinner on the Cross, and therefore He was punished on the Cross. Some even teach that Jesus had to go to hell for three days to pay for those sins, and after He had paid for His sins, He was allowed to rise from the dead. None of that is true.

On the Cross, Jesus had to be the spotless Lamb, the perfect sacrifice. On the Cross He was still without blemish. He was holy in eternity before He became human, then He lived a holy life, and He remains holy in eternity now. To remain fully God as well as fully human, Christ had to remain holy, undefiled, and separate from sinners. He is the one who knew no sin, period! He is not merely one who knew no sin until the Cross.

When the Bible says that Christ was made sin it means it only in one sense—that God treated Him as if He were a sinner, even though He was not. Let me be more specific. On the Cross, God treated Jesus as if He had personally committed every sin committed by every person who would ever believe in Him, even though in fact He had committed none of them. That's what substitution means. Jesus was our substitute, taking our punishment. As Isaiah 53 already showed us, God put the punishment for our sins on Him, even though He was the sinless Son of God.

The rest of the verse tells us the reason Christ was made sin for us. It was so that we might become the righteousness of God in Him. That's the other side of substitution. God treated Jesus as if He were a sinner so that He could treat us as if we were righteous.

Have you ever wondered why Jesus had to come into the world and live 33 years when we have almost no information about His first 30 years? Why did He have to bother with those 30 years? If I had been God, I might have said, "Son, I need you to go down and die for the sins of all who will ever believe. It should only take a weekend. Just go down on Friday so you can be crucified, come out of the grave on Sunday, and you can come back." If His whole purpose was only about death and resurrection, what were the first 30 years about?

Here's the answer: Jesus said when He was being baptized by John that He must fulfill all righteousness. He was doing that all through his life—living a perfectly righteous life. Hebrews 4:15 says that He was tempted in all points like as we are, yet without sin. He was tempted as a child, as a young person, and as an adult—and yet He did not sin.

Why did He have to live that sinless life? So that His sinless life could be credited to your account. That is the doctrine of substitution—that Jesus' sinlessness could be given to you, or "imputed" to you. On the Cross, God treated Jesus as if He lived your life, so that God can treat you as if you lived Jesus' life. That is the heart of the gospel.

TAKING *away the* CHARGES AGAINST US

> And you, being dead in your trespasses and the uncircumcision of your flesh, He has made alive together with Him, having forgiven you all trespasses, having wiped out the handwriting of requirements that was against us, which was contrary to us. And He has taken it out of the way, having nailed it to the cross.
>
> —*Colossians 2:13–14* NKJV

You were dead because of your sins and because your sinful nature was not yet cut away. Then God made you alive with Christ. He forgave all our sins. He canceled the record that contained the charges against us. He took it and destroyed it by nailing it to Christ's cross.

—*Colossians 2:13–14 NLT*

These verses portray a very vivid image, even if the language is difficult to understand. Paul uses legal concepts from the ancient world. When a person was crucified, the list of his crimes would be nailed to the cross to make obvious to everyone the reason he was being punished. When Jesus was crucified, the soldiers nailed a sign on the Cross saying, "This is Jesus of Nazareth, the King of the Jews." The indictment against Jesus was that He was a king, a rebel against the Roman emperor, and an offense to Jews who were looking for a very different kind of king. This was the crime for which He was being put to death.

Paul takes that image of the indictment and says the list of charges against us was nailed to the Cross as well. All the laws we had broken, all the requirements we had failed to meet that were now "against us," were nailed by God to the Cross. The list of our sins was posted there, but we did not have to die for them. Jesus died for them in our stead.

Paul says that before that, we were spiritually dead in our trespasses. We were "uncircumcised"—

unclean and not part of God's people. But now all that has changed. We have been forgiven all our sins because Jesus paid the penalty for them on the Cross. We are no longer dead; we've been made alive with Christ because the death penalty we were under has been fulfilled.

All the charges against us have been dropped, because the penalty has already been carried out. We have been declared innocent, not because we deserve it, but because all our offenses against God have been placed on Jesus Christ, who satisfies God the righteous Judge. We can never thank or praise Him enough for dying to give us life.

REDEEMING US *with* HIS BLOOD

> Knowing that you were not redeemed with corruptible things, like silver or gold, from your aimless conduct received by tradition from your fathers, but with the precious blood of Christ, as of a lamb without blemish and without spot.
> —*1 Peter 1:18–19*

We sing that we are "redeemed by the blood of the Lamb." Those are tremendous concepts that are difficult for many twenty-first century people to understand. But they are critical to the meaning of what happened on the Cross.

Redemption was a technical term for money paid to buy back a prisoner of war. That is what God did for us when Jesus died for us. Peter says that we needed to be set free from the useless, aimless life passed down by tradition from our fathers, just living in the way of the world. We were trapped in this corrupt world system, running in the rat race, going through the motions of living, without really living the way God intended. We needed to be rescued from that old way of life, because in the end it leads to death and God's judgment.

But how could we be redeemed? Nothing in this world could purchase our freedom—not silver or gold or any earthly commodity. Only one thing could redeem us. Peter says it was the precious blood of Jesus Christ.

The only way for us to be set free from our old way of life and its consequences was for a sacrifice—a substitute acceptable to God—to be found. Throughout the Old Testament the Israelites sacrificed lambs and other animals in the temple as sin offerings, to take away the sin of the people. That entire system looked forward to the coming of the Lord Jesus Christ, who would be the ultimate Lamb. He would be the perfect, final sacrifice, the Lamb without blemish and without spot.

A generation after the death of Jesus, the city of Jerusalem and the temple were destroyed by the Romans, just as Jesus had predicted. With the destruction of the temple in A.D. 70, the entire sacrificial system came to an end. From that day until now, there has never been a temple and there has never been a place to offer sacrifices. None is needed. Jesus was the final sacrifice. He paid, once for all, for the sins of every person who would ever believe. He paid the price to redeem us, to set us free, with His own blood.

Now you know—and can share—the *why* of the Cross.

CHAPTER 5

ACCEPTING GOD'S SALVATION

AT THE HEART OF THE BIBLE—in some of our favorite verses—is the truth that God wants us to accept the gift of salvation. It is not enough to believe, as we saw in chapter 3, that God is sovereign over everything. That would be a frightening thought if we did not also believe that the almighty God's desire is to save us rather than see us destroyed. It is not enough to know what happened on the Cross. It is possible to know that God paid a price for our salvation and yet refuse the gift. Scripture says that we must believe in the One who died for us, accepting by faith the free gift of salvation, confessing our faith before others, and committing ourselves to Jesus as Lord.

How *to* Escape Perishing

> For God so loved the world that He gave
> His only begotten Son, that whoever
> believes in Him should not perish but
> have everlasting life. For God did not send
> His Son into the world to condemn the
> world, but that the world through Him
> might be saved.
>
> —*John 3:16–17*

This may be one of the first verses you ever memorized. What a wonderful truth! God wants us to know that there is a way to escape perishing. To understand the reason God gave His Son, you have to understand the kind of world into which He sent Him. It was a world where people were perishing. God did not send His Son to condemn the world, because the world was already condemned. He sent his Son to save people who were perishing.

That word "perish" jumps out at us. It means more than just to die physically. It connotes everlasting destruction and divine punishment—in a word, hell. Jesus said more about hell than He did about heaven. He talked about a fire that is never quenched, about a place where the worm never dies, where people gnash their teeth and weep and wail, where there is utter darkness. That is what it means to perish.

But God so loved the world that He sent His Son so that we don't have to perish. We can have everlasting life—or more exactly, eternal life. It is not just the kind of life we have now, going on and on forever. None of us could endure that; it would be a kind of hell. Eternal life is a different kind of life. It is not just a change in the quantity of life, but the quality of life. We are given God's kind of life. We participate in the bliss of divine immortality, in the very life that belongs to God Himself. God gives us His own life which exists eternally within the Father and the Son and the Holy Spirit. He rescues us from perishing and He gives us eternal life.

Who is it that receives this life? Whoever believes in God's only begotten Son. Jesus says that those who come to Him He will never turn away (John 6:37). Whoever believes in Him will be saved. What does it mean to believe in Him? It does not merely mean to believe that a person named Jesus once lived in history. It means to believe that Jesus is who He said He was. To believe in Jesus means to believe in the true Jesus:

the Jesus who is God incarnate,
the Jesus who was born of a virgin,
the Jesus who lived a sinless life,
the Jesus who died a substitutionary death on the Cross,
the Jesus who was raised from the dead,
the Jesus who ascended into heaven,
the Jesus who now intercedes at the right hand of the Father as our great High Priest,

the Jesus who has been declared Lord by God Himself,

the Jesus who will come someday to gather His own to Himself and establish the glory of His eternal kingdom.

Believing in *that* Jesus is the only way to escape perishing. Paul warned that others might come preaching another Jesus (2 Corinthians 11:4), and that those who preach another gospel should be accursed (Galatians 1:8). But those who believe in the true Jesus are *not* condemned. They are rescued from perishing by the love of God.

How *to* Be Saved

> That if you confess with your mouth the Lord Jesus and believe in your heart that God has raised Him from the dead, you will be saved. For with the heart one believes unto righteousness, and with the mouth confession is made unto salvation.
>
> —*Romans 10:9–10*

This critical portion of Scripture lays out the two things you must do to be saved. What could be more important?

The first thing you must do is to confess with your mouth Jesus as Lord. This means more than acknowledging that Jesus is *the* Lord, more than

THE HEART OF THE BIBLE

saying that Jesus is God. After all, James 2:19 says that even demons know that God is the sovereign of the universe, but that knowledge does not save them.

Confessing Jesus as Lord means saying that Jesus is *your* Lord, *your* Sovereign. Making this confession means expressing out loud before others your deep personal conviction—without reservation—that Jesus is your Master and the Ruler of your life.

Jesus said, "If you want to follow me, you must deny yourself" (Luke 9:23). That is an amazing statement, considering the way people think about the role of Jesus in their lives today. The gospel is not about self-fulfillment, as many suppose. It is about self-denial. No one can confess Jesus as Lord and say, "OK, Jesus, I'm going to let you into my life and I want you to make me more successful and improve my marriage and lower my golf handicap." The gospel is not about Jesus coming into your life and giving you what you want. It is about you coming before Jesus and saying, "God, be merciful to me, a sinner. Save me." It is about saying, "Jesus, I acknowledge You as my Sovereign, Master, and Lord. I turn away from my own desires and my own need to control my life. I submit to whatever You want for me."

The rich young ruler would not do that (Luke 18:18–27). Jesus told him to do one thing: sell everything you have and give it to the poor, then follow me. You aren't saved by getting rid of your money. Jesus' point was to test the man's commitment to Jesus as his Lord. He could have asked him to do a hundred different things, but Jesus chose something He knew would test his willingness to deny himself. The ruler could not bring himself to submit to Jesus' rule over him. He could not confess in this way that Jesus was the Lord of his life. He went away sad—and unsaved.

The second thing you must do to be saved is believe in your heart that God raised Jesus from the dead. Belief in the Resurrection means that you also believe that Jesus died on the Cross and was raised from the dead as the sign that He really is the Messiah, raised ultimately to the highest place to rule with the Father. God the Father put the stamp of divine approval on the perfect work of Jesus— His sinless life and His substitutionary death— when He raised Him from the dead. The Resurrection was the supreme validation of His ministry and His identity.

You will be saved only when you have acknowledged Jesus as your Lord and believed that His death on the Cross was indeed the effective sacrifice for your sin, validated by His glorious resurrection. You believe with your heart and are made right with God; you confess with your mouth and confirm that reality.

Saved *by* Grace

For by grace you have been saved through
faith, and that not of yourselves; it is the
gift of God, not of works, lest anyone
should boast.

—*Ephesians 2:8–9*

These verses clarify the work of salvation: it is all
God's doing, and not our own. We are saved by
God's grace by means of faith. It is all the gift of
God. We are not saved by our good works, so we
have no reason to be proud, as if being a Christian
were an achievement. The only way to be saved is by
grace, which is God's unmerited favor. If we
deserved it, it would not be grace. We are not saved
because we have been good enough, because we
have done the right things, or earned salvation in
any way.

The Bible is clear that we cannot earn our
salvation. Paul wrote in Romans 3:20, "By the deeds
of the law no flesh will be justified." He wrote in
Galatians 3:10 that those who rely on good works to
be saved are under a curse, because everyone who
breaks God's law is under a curse and none of us
can keep that law. We are all justifiably doomed to
eternal punishment unless God intervenes by grace.
That is just what God has done.

God brings salvation to us by grace, and our
response is faith. But even our faith does not come
from ourselves. "That not of yourselves" refers not

only to the grace but also the faith. We are required to believe to be saved, but since we are dead in sin we can't believe. The natural man cannot understand spiritual truths (1 Corinthians 2:14), so he cannot believe. The god of this world (the devil) has blinded the minds of unbelievers so that the light of the gospel cannot shine on them (2 Corinthians 4:4). So there we are before we are saved—in the dark, dead in our sin, blind to the truth, having no hope and without God (Ephesians 2:12). We are helpless, unable to generate faith from our dead hearts.

God has to bring our dead hearts to life. God has to give sight to our blind eyes. God has to give understanding to our darkened minds. The whole work of salvation, then, is a miracle of God. We do believe the gospel and receive the Lord Jesus Christ by faith, but it is God who gives us the desire, the ability, and the understanding to do just that. None of us can boast about our faith or our salvation, because it is all due to God's grace from beginning to end.

Good News *for the* Burdened

> Come to Me, all you who labor and are heavy laden, and I will give you rest. Take My yoke upon you and learn from Me, for I am gentle and lowly in heart, and you will find rest for your souls. For My yoke is easy and My burden is light.
>
> —*Matthew 11:28–30*

These words of Jesus came as wonderfully good news to the people who heard them. They were laboring under a heavy burden. It was the burden of trying to earn their salvation by keeping the law and all the ordinances and traditions that had developed in the Judaism of that time. Jesus said in Matthew 23:4 that the teachers of the law and the Pharisees laid heavy burdens on the people but would never lift a finger to help them carry the load. Trying to be good enough to make yourself right with God is a heavy burden that no one can bear. Yet even today there are many, many people around the world laboring under that burden. Every system of salvation by works is an impossible system, because the Scripture says that no one can be justified by the deeds of the law (Romans 3:20) and you can be saved only by grace, not by works.

There may be many religions in the world, but there are only two systems of salvation. There is the truth of the gospel—that salvation comes apart from works as the free gift of God by grace through faith. Then there is every other system, by whatever name, that says you can earn your way to heaven by religious ceremony, by moral deeds, or by good works. That is a lie from the devil, to make us trust ourselves rather than God. That is the deception most of the world labors under, and it is a heavy burden. A religion of works can provide no peace and no rest, because no one can be perfect. No one can rise above his or her fallenness.

But Jesus came along and said, "Come to me, all of you who are laboring under the immense burden of trying to earn your salvation, and I will give you rest. Instead of this yoke of the law and tradition that has been placed on you like a rough wooden yoke that an ox wears to pull an impossibly heavy cart, take my yoke. I am gentle. I am lowly in heart. I will give you rest, because my yoke is easy and my burden is light."

That is the wonderful promise of salvation by grace through faith. Salvation is effortless on our part, because the great effort was made by Jesus Christ in His death and resurrection. Because He has already accomplished our salvation, we now have rest—rest from trying to earn salvation by our own works.

A Hymn of Salvation

And without controversy great is the mystery of godliness:
God was manifested in the flesh,
Justified in the Spirit,
Seen by angels,
Preached among the Gentiles,
Believed on in the world,
Received up in glory.
                                    —*1 Timothy 3:16*

This verse is part of an early church hymn, a fact that is evident from its uniformity, rhythm, and parallelism in Greek. Its six lines form a concise summary of the gospel. The mystery of godliness is the secret of God's nature and plan that was hidden for many ages and has now been revealed in Jesus Christ. When Paul talked about mystery, he always meant some great truth that was obscure in the Old Testament but had now been made clear. The greatest of all mysteries was the mystery of God becoming human flesh, the mystery of Jesus Himself, the glorious reality of the Incarnation.

The Incarnation becomes a sort of theme for this hymn. God was manifested in the flesh through the miracle of the Virgin Birth. The phrase "justified in the Spirit" does not actually refer to the Holy Spirit, but means rather that Jesus was righteous in His spirit, in His inner person. When God became a human being He was perfectly righteous, perfectly holy. "Seen by angels" means that all the angels— holy angels and fallen angels—acknowledged Jesus as the incarnate One. The holy angels sang at His birth and ministered to Him after His temptation. The fallen angels (demons) acknowledged Jesus as the Holy One of God, although they were afraid of him and said, "What have we to do with you?" (Mark 1:24).

Jesus was "preached among the Gentiles"—or more accurately, "among the nations." The apostles took the glorious message of Jesus Christ and began to spread it to the ends of the earth as He had commanded. He was "believed on in the world." There were many who believed. After the Resurrection He appeared to 500 in Galilee. When he appeared in the Upper Room in Judea, there were 120 believers there. On the day of Pentecost more than 3,000 from around the world believed on Him. Soon there were thousands and thousands more, and now the gospel has spread to every part of the world.

Finally the hymn says "He was received up in glory." The gospel message is not complete without saying that Jesus ascended to the highest place and was received in glory in heaven, where He now sits at the right hand of the Father.

THREE PHASES *of* SALVATION

> Being confident of this very thing, that He who has begun a good work in you will complete it until the day of Jesus Christ.
> —*Philippians 1:6*

The work that God has begun in you is the work of salvation. When God begins that work in a person, He finishes it. Paul once said something surprising about salvation: "Now our salvation is nearer than when we first believed" (Romans 13:11). How can that be? Didn't we receive our salvation when we first believed? Yes, we did,

THE HEART OF THE BIBLE

but Paul is talking about the completion of our salvation when Jesus comes again and we are transformed.

For the Christian there are three phases of salvation. Part is in the past when Jesus died on the Cross and you subsequently believed in Him. Part is in the present as the Spirit continually works in your life to change you and set you free from sin. Part is in the future as we expect to be changed completely and enjoy eternal life in heaven. The first phase is justification, which happens when you repent and put your faith in Christ and are made right with God. The second phase is sanctification, as you are gradually separated from sin. The third phase is glorification, which will occur when we leave this world and enter heaven and are freed from the old fallen flesh and its influences. At that point we will be free of the reality of sin entirely and able to enter into the full perfection and absolute holiness of eternal life.

As a Christian, you have already been justified and forgiven. You are in the process of being sanctified, being progressively set apart from sin by the work of the Holy Spirit through the Word. One day you will be glorified, made like Jesus Christ, as much as glorified humanity can be like incarnate deity. We give thanks for the gift of salvation we have already received, but we rejoice to know that God has only just begun to change us, and He will finish what He started.

We pray the words of Charles Wesley's hymn:

Finish then Thy new creation,
pure and spotless let us be;
Let us see Thy great salvation perfectly
restored in Thee:
Changed from glory into glory,
till in heaven we take our place,
Till we cast our crowns before Thee,
lost in wonder, love, and praise!

CHAPTER 6

MORE THAN WE DESERVE

∞

THE HEART OF THE BIBLE reveals the very heart of God. Of all the amazing things we discover about God in the Old and New Testaments, the most amazing is this—that the heart of God is full of love and mercy. It is not what we really expect, deep down, and it is not what we deserve. We know that we are guilty, so we harbor deep suspicions that God wants to punish us. But the truth Scripture reveals is that God wants to forgive us if we will only repent.

When Moses asked to see God's face—to know God's nature intimately—God agreed to show Moses his back, as it were, giving him an indirect view of His glory. When God passed by, this is how He identified Himself: "I am the LORD, I am the LORD, the merciful and gracious God. I am slow to

anger and rich in unfailing love and faithfulness"
(Exodus 34:6 NLT).

Jesus both taught and demonstrated that God
is the merciful and gracious Father who receives
sinners. As we have seen in chapter 4, He
demonstrated His love in that while we were still
sinners, Christ died for us. This forgiving love is so
central to God's nature that John can say "God is
love" (1 John 4:8). No matter how long we are
Christians, this continues to surprise us because we
are so undeserving. That is why we continue to sing
of God's amazing love and amazing grace.

Unfailing Compassion

> Through the LORD's mercies we are not
> consumed, because His compassions fail
> not. They are new every morning; great is
> Your faithfulness.
> —*Lamentations 3:22–23*

It is only through the Lord's mercies that we are
not consumed. Mercy means withholding what we
deserve, not giving us the punishment we deserve.
The fact is that we do deserve punishment. We
deserve God's judgment because we have broken
His law, because we have spurned His love, because
we have offended and dishonored Him. We do that
every time we sin. We should be consumed by His
justice, but His justice is tempered by His mercy.

His mercy is based on His compassion for us and that compassion never fails.

When I was rearing my children, there were times I showed mercy as a parent, but I cannot say I had absolutely unfailing compassion. Looking back, I can see that there were times when I ran out of compassion. Like most parents, I did not always demonstrate the forgiving love of God when I could have. Because I am human and fallen, my compassion failed. But the Lord tells us that His compassions never fail. His mercy is never diminished by fatigue or irritation or time. As Paul tells us in Romans 5:20, where sin abounds, grace abounds much more. Even when we continue to sin, God's grace abounds.

These acts of compassion toward us are new every morning. God never runs out of His supply of compassion. Every day is a new day with Him. What a wonderful thing to think about at the start of the day! It is a new day and all the mercies and compassions of God are available for that day.

Why does God have such mercy and compassion? Why is the supply new today even though yesterday was a bad day or a disappointing day or a sinful day? Here is why: Great is Your faithfulness. The bedrock of God's mercy and compassion is His covenant. When God makes a promise, He keeps it. During Israel's forty years of wandering in the desert and all through the Scriptures, God has promised us mercy and compassion if we trust in

Him. God is always faithful to Himself and His Word. God cannot lie and cannot break a promise. Second Timothy 2:13 says, "If we are faithless, He remains faithful; He cannot deny Himself."

We wake every new day, no matter what the prior day held, engulfed in the mercy and compassion of a God who keeps His covenant even to His failing children.

TALKING *to* YOURSELF

> Bless the LORD, O my soul; and all that is within me, bless His holy name! Bless the LORD, O my soul, and forget not all His benefits: Who forgives all your iniquities, Who heals all your diseases, Who redeems your life from destruction, Who crowns you with lovingkindness and tender mercies.
>
> —*Psalm 103:1–4*

We all talk to ourselves. You probably told yourself this morning, "Self, get out of bed." You told yourself to open this book. We all engage in self-talk, and Psalm 103 gives us a model for the right kind of self-talk. Consider this model: "Soul, bless the Lord. Self, praise God. Everything that is in me, bless His holy name." Get into the habit of telling yourself to bless God, and train your soul to bless His name.

How do you train your soul to bless God? By remembering His benefits. Remember what God has done for you. Count your blessings. When things go wrong in your life you might forget His benefits. When you are disappointed you might forget His blessings. But nothing that happens in this life can affect God's eternal blessing on you as His child.

What are the benefits listed here? First, God forgives all your sins. What a place to start! Second, God heals all your diseases. Every healing you have experienced came from God. Some diseases will not be healed in time but in eternity; if they are not healed in this life they will be healed in heaven as you are made absolutely perfect. Third, He has already redeemed your life from destruction and set you free from the power of death. Fourth, on top of all that, God has crowned you with love and mercy. That word "lovingkindness" is the Hebrew word *hesed*. It means God's "covenant love" and is the Old Testament word for "grace." God's tender mercy toward you as a sinner is the theme of Psalm 103— He pours out that love and mercy on you. Your response to that is to praise His holy name with everything that is in you.

Things do go wrong in this life. Murphy's Law seems to be operating—that whatever can go wrong, will. But nothing ever goes wrong in the eternal kingdom. Nothing ever goes wrong in the purposes of God and you can count on them.

God's purpose is to bless you, to forgive you, to heal you, to redeem you, and to love you. That is why you can say to yourself, "Bless the LORD, O my soul; and all that is within me, bless His holy name!"

THE SHADOW *of* DEATH

The LORD is my shepherd; I shall not want.
He makes me to lie down in green pastures;
He leads me beside the still waters.
He restores my soul;
He leads me in the paths of righteousness
    for His name's sake.
Yea, though I walk through the valley of
    the shadow of death,
I will fear no evil;
For You are with me; Your rod and Your
    staff, they comfort me.
You prepare a table before me in the
    presence of my enemies;
You anoint my head with oil; my cup runs
    over.
Surely goodness and mercy shall follow
    me all the days of my life;
And I will dwell in the house of the LORD
    forever.

—Psalm 23

This psalm gives us a memorable picture of God's goodness and mercy demonstrated in His constant care for His people. Books have been written on the great truths in this familiar shepherd's song, but I will focus on just one image. It is the one that jumps out at us when we hear this psalm read at funerals: "Yea, though I walk through the valley of the shadow of death, I will fear no evil; for Thou art with me" (KJV).

Sheep are not capable of leading themselves. They need to be led by a shepherd to find food, and the Lord is the Shepherd who feeds us. Sheep need to be led to still waters, because the rushing waters of streams and rivers will sweep them away and they cannot drink from them. Sheep need to be led to safety. They need to be protected by the shepherd's rod and staff when they are threatened by deadly peril—when they are in the shadow of death.

As believers, we never walk through the valley of death; we walk through the valley of the *shadow* of death. What do you think the psalmist meant by that? A famous story told of the great preacher Donald Grey Barnhouse offers insight.

The death of Dr Barnhouse's wife left him and a six-year-old daughter in the home. He had real difficulty working through his own grief, but the hardest part was to comfort and explain the death to his daughter. One day they were standing on a busy corner at a downtown intersection waiting for a light to change. Suddenly a very large truck sped by the corner, briefly blocking out the sun and frightening the daughter. To comfort her, Dr. Barnhouse picked her up, and in a moment, the wisdom of God broke through and he was able to explain to her: "When you saw the truck pass, it scared you, but let me ask you, had you rather be struck by the truck or the shadow of the truck?"

She replied, "Of course, the shadow."

He went on to explain that when "your mother died, she was only hit by the shadow of death because Jesus was hit by the truck (death)" [James Hewett, *Illustrations Unlimited*, Wheaton: Tyndale House, 1988, p. 148]. Mrs. Barnhouse only went through the valley of the shadow of death, so we fear no evil for her.

Death is but a harmless shadow for the sheep of the Good Shepherd. As the apostle Paul exclaims, "O death, where is your victory? O death, where is your sting?... Thanks be to God, who gives us the victory through our Lord Jesus Christ" (1 Corinthians 15:55, 57 NASB). The Good Shepherd protects us from death. All the days of our lives His goodness and mercy pursue us, as He cares for us, feeds us, and puts oil on our wounds. One day He will bring us into His eternal house forever.

NOTHING CAN SEPARATE US

> For I am persuaded that neither death nor
> life, nor angels nor principalities nor
> powers, nor things present nor things to
> come, nor height nor depth, nor
> any other created thing, shall be able to
> separate us from the love of God which is
> in Christ Jesus our Lord.
> —*Romans 8:38–39*

The apostle Paul could have written simply, "Nothing can separate us from the love of God which is in Christ Jesus our Lord." But somebody would have said, "Oh, but what about this? What about that? Can't these things separate us from God's love?"

So for the sake of those people, Paul makes a comprehensive list. "I am persuaded," he says in the strongest terms—completely convinced, absolutely sure—that none of these things can come between us and God's love. He starts with death, because that is the first thing we are afraid will cut us off from God. No, not death, he says; and no, not life. Those are the only two possibilities. In either case, you cannot be separated from God's love.

Then Paul moves to the realm of spirit beings we might be afraid of, holy ones and unholy ones. Neither angels nor demons ("principalities nor powers") have the power to cut us off from God's love. We do not need to live in fear of them.

Then he moves to the dimension of time. Nothing in the present and nothing in the future can take you out of God's covenant of love. Then he moves to the dimension of space. There is nothing up to the highest point in the universe, and nothing down to the lowest point that can get between you and God's love.

If that is not enough, Paul adds one more thing. There isn't any created thing that can separate you from His love, and everything in the universe except God is a created thing. There is absolutely nothing that can separate you from the love of God. That includes you, since you are a created thing. There is nothing you can do that will ever separate you from God's love. No demonic power or angelic power can do it. I don't care if it's something in the present or something in the future that you are worried about. I don't care whether it is something real or imagined. There is nothing that exists that can change your eternal relationship to God if you are in Christ Jesus our Lord.

Some may say this verse is a wonderful encouragement. Others, though, will say it merely encourages people to run out and sin. I believe that just the opposite is true. The knowledge of God's gracious love in Christ draws us to Him and changes us. It produces worship and obedience, not rebellion. The Holy Spirit works in us as believers to conform us to the image of Jesus Christ.

You can know that this promise is true: You are among "those who are called, sanctified by God the Father, and preserved in Jesus Christ" (Jude 1). The One who justified you will also sanctify you and will one day glorify you. This is because God loves you with an everlasting love and you are hidden with Christ in God's love. A glorious future awaits you, not because you deserve it, but because God is faithful to His everlasting love.

His Grace Is Sufficient

> And He said to me, "My grace is sufficient for you, for My strength is made perfect in weakness." Therefore most gladly I will rather boast in my infirmities, that the power of Christ may rest upon me. Therefore I take pleasure in infirmities, in reproaches, in needs, in persecutions, in distresses, for Christ's sake. For when I am weak, then I am strong.
> —*2 Corinthians 12:9–10*

Paul certainly goes against the grain of our culture! Can you imagine someone saying that weakness is better than strength? Can you imagine celebrities boasting in their infirmities? Paul says, "I take pleasure in infirmities, reproaches, needs, persecutions, in distresses." He sounds like a masochist. Why would he say something like that?

Because God has a purpose in all these painful experiences in life.

Paul had many painful experiences, including one chronic source of pain he referred to as "a thorn in the flesh." He asked the Lord three times to take it away, but He declined to do it. Instead, He said to Paul, "My grace is sufficient." My grace is enough for you. My love and mercy will get you through.

Every difficult time in our lives—every infirmity, reproach, need, persecution, distress—is an opportunity for God to manifest His sufficient grace. Every time of weakness is an opportunity for Christ to demonstrate His power. I have learned that over and over. When my son had a brain tumor it was a horrible experience from a human standpoint. But I went through a nine-day fast, praying for my son, and I experienced grace beyond description. It was one of the spiritual highlights of my entire life. When my wife had an automobile accident and broke her neck, it was a terrible ordeal but once again I found that His grace was sufficient.

You never experience that grace until you need it. You may wonder how you are going to do when you face death. If you are a Christian, I can tell you how you will do—you'll do fine. I've seen it thousands of times. At the moment when you need it, His grace will be enough for you. But you will not receive that grace until that moment.

The Lord also said to Paul, "My strength is made perfect in [your] weakness." What does that mean?

THE HEART OF THE BIBLE

It means that when you go through the kinds of trials in life that you just can't fix, you become dependent on His strength rather than your own. I used to encourage people to trust God for something so big that when it happened they would know that only God could have done it. Well, sometimes God brings those big things into our lives. God brings problems into our lives that only He can fix, issues that only He can change, so that we are left in situations of weakness and helplessness. In those times, the strength that we find is God's strength and not our own. If God fixes those problems or addresses those issues, we can be sure that it was Him and not us.

Suffering is an opportunity for God to display His grace and power. Accept your weakness. No one is too weak to be made powerful, but many are too strong. If you embrace your suffering, you will see the grace and strength of God perfected in your life.

SATISFACTION

In this the love of God was manifested toward us, that God has sent His only begotten Son into the world, that we might live through Him. In this is love, not that we loved God, but that He loved us and sent His Son to be the propitiation for our sins.

—*1 John 4:9–10*

God's love and grace were demonstrated to us in our weakness when He sent His Son into the world to give us life. We were dead in our sins, but we were made alive in Christ. This is how we know what real love is—not by our experience of loving God, but by Christ's death on the Cross for us. God defined love for us by giving Himself in the form of His Son as a sacrifice, the propitiation for our sins.

What does "propitiation" mean? It means satisfaction. Jesus came to be the satisfaction for our sins. Who had to be satisfied? God had to be satisfied, because God had been offended by our sin, which violated His law. Sin is an act of rebellion against God, violating His honor and justice. If God is to forgive a sinner, His justice must be satisfied. Jesus came to do that by His sinless life and His substitutionary death. The sacrificial death of the innocent One satisfied the divine justice.

God was perfectly satisfied with His Son. Do you remember what the voice from heaven said when Jesus was baptized? "This is My beloved Son in Whom I am well pleased" (Matthew 3:17). The same voice came when Jesus was transfigured: "This is My beloved Son in Whom I am well pleased" (Matthew 17:5). The Father was perfectly satisfied with His Son so that His Son could be the perfect satisfaction for our sins.

Such truths about how God's love satisfied His justice within Himself can seem rather abstract. Let me bring it down to a personal level. How satisfied are you with Jesus? That is such a basic spiritual question to ask yourself. The Father is perfectly satisfied with the Son; the Son is perfectly satisfied with the Father. How about you? Are you perfectly satisfied with Jesus Christ? Is He your deepest and truest satisfaction? Do you find your highest joy in Him? Where you look for satisfaction and joy will shape your whole life. God is most pleased with us when we are most satisfied with His Son.

CHAPTER 7

LIVING WORTHY
of OUR CALLING

WE HAVE SEEN OVER AND OVER in key passages that the heart of the Bible lies in God's gracious offer of salvation, which comes to us not on the basis of our worthiness, but on the basis of His love and mercy. But it is also true that salvation produces a worthy life. Justification leads to sanctification. Second Timothy 1:9 (NIV) says that God "saved us and called us to a holy life—not because of anything we have done but because of his own purpose and grace." Paul urges the Ephesians "to walk worthy of the calling with which you were called" (4:1). Our calling to salvation is meant to produce a life of Christian character and purity.

WHO MAY COME *into* GOD'S PRESENCE?

> Who may ascend into the hill of the
> LORD? Or who may stand in His holy
> place? He who has clean hands and a pure
> heart, who has not lifted up his soul to
> an idol, nor sworn deceitfully. He
> shall receive blessing from the LORD,
> and righteousness from the God of his
> salvation.
>
> —*Psalm 24:3–5*

I have stood in the city of Jerusalem on the south
side of the Temple Mount. The place of worship
once stood on top of that large hill. You can still see
the steps that led up through the wall to the temple
where the Jewish people, including Jesus, went up
to worship until the destruction of the temple in
70 A.D. In order to worship, they ascended the hill of
the Lord.

It is likely that in ancient times the priests would
ask the worshipers as they approached the hill:
"Who may ascend into the hill of the LORD? Or who
may stand in His holy place?" The people would
answer antiphonally: "He who has clean hands and
a pure heart, who has not lifted up his soul to
an idol, nor sworn deceitfully." They knew the
qualifications for drawing near to God. They could
not come into the holy place if they were unclean
with unforgiven sin in their lives. They could not
approach God with divided hearts. They could not

lift up their praises to the God of Israel if they had already praised a false god. They could not draw near to pledge allegiance to the Lord if they had used His name in false oaths. The priests asked the questions to remind the people to examine their hearts as they came to worship.

I wonder if we ever really ask ourselves such questions when we come to worship. We are focused on music and performance and welcoming people, but do we ever ask who has the right to worship? Do I have a right to come rushing into the presence of the holy God? A church building is not the temple in Jerusalem, but God is there, because He inhabits the praises of His people (Psalm 22:3 KJV). Do I have a right to "ascend" into His presence?

I have no right unless I come with clean hands and a pure heart. I have no right if there are idols in my soul or if I am swearing allegiance to Him deceitfully. You may think you would never do that, but if you sing "I love you, Lord," and you do not love Him with all your heart, you are swearing allegiance to Him deceitfully. When you sing hymns of devotion, you are pledging your loyalty to God. Are you holding anything back? Are there impurities or idols in your heart? If that is the case, you will not receive blessing from the Lord or the mercies of His righteousness.

We no longer climb the Temple Mount because God does not dwell in a temple made with hands.

Those who worship Him must worship Him in spirit and in truth (John 4:24). Every time we worship—whether it is in a sanctuary or a school gym or outdoors—we go though the veil into the Most Holy Place. We stand in the presence of God. If you could see God's presence and had to pass through a literal veil, you would not think of doing it unless you had dealt with the sin in your life. Why, then, would you walk right into His invisible presence without dealing with your sin? Make sure your heart is right as you enter His presence, because God wants to pour out His blessing and give you the gift of His righteousness.

BEING ALIVE *in* MORTAL BODIES

> Therefore do not let sin reign in your mortal body, that you should obey it in its lusts. And do not present your members as instruments of unrighteousness to sin, but present yourselves to God as being alive from the dead, and your members as instruments of righteousness to God.
> —*Romans 6:12–13*

When you come to Christ, you are made a new creation (2 Corinthians 5:7). You are given a new nature—a new disposition with new longings and desires. You want to do what is right and you are no longer under the unbroken dominion of sin. But even though you are new on the inside, that new nature is still incarcerated in fallen humanness. That is what Paul is talking about when he says that we are alive from the dead, and yet find ourselves in mortal bodies. The only part of us that is vulnerable to sin is these bodies destined for death, both their parts ("members") and their lusts.

That struggle between the influence of sin and our new nature will go on as long as we live in these bodies. That is why Paul says in Romans 8:23 that we eagerly await the redemption of our bodies. Someday we will be completely free of sin, but right now there is a battle. Like Paul, we do things that we hate, and we don't do things we want to. In this battle we are commanded not to let sin take over. Do not obey the enemy. Don't report for duty to sin, offering your body parts to sin as instruments of unrighteousness. Instead, report for duty to God, offering your body parts as instruments of righteousness, to be used on the right side of this ongoing battle. You can make the decision to offer yourself to God. You can fill your mind with biblical truth. You can discipline your body and bring it into subjection (1 Corinthians 9:27). And you can hold on to the hope of heaven and being free at last.

When I think about heaven, I am curious about what I'll see there. I want to see a gate that is made of one large pearl and streets of transparent gold. I am curious about the New Jerusalem shaped like a cube and the light of God's glory blazing out of the center of the throne through multicolored jewels, diffusing light all over the universe. I am curious to see what I will be like and what my loved ones are going to be like, but when we are perfect we may not recognize each other. Most of all I look forward to seeing Jesus Christ face to face.

But do you know that what appeals to me most about heaven is the absence of sin? I'm much more eager to have sin out of my life than I am to sit on a cloud or see the sights of heaven. I want the battle to be over. The promise of Scripture is that the battle will be over soon, and that the victory is already won. Someday we will be set free from these mortal bodies, transformed into the likeness of Christ's glorious body. Sin will be no more. Until then, we battle, and we offer ourselves to God as His instruments for His righteous purposes.

The Fruit *of the* Spirit

> But the fruit of the Spirit is love, joy, peace, longsuffering, kindness, goodness, faithfulness, gentleness, self-control. Against such there is no law.
> —*Galatians 5:22–23*

When the Spirit of God is in full control of your life, this is what you are going to be like. These nine attitudes are interlinked. They come in a package as what the fruit the Spirit produces. These attitudes are not like the gifts of the Spirit; you do not each receive one or more of these attitudes based on your temperament. If you are under the control of the Holy Spirit, living in obedience to the Word of God, then all nine of these attitudes will be produced in your life. That godly character is the evidence that the Holy Spirit—not your old fallen nature—is in control.

There is no such thing as a partial package of the fruit of the Spirit. It is not like the mail order "fruit of the month" clubs where you can order grapefruit but skip the oranges and take the pears but pass on the apples. You receive all nine characteristics in one package. It could never be true that a person walking in the Spirit, under His control, would have love but no joy, or peace but no patience, or kindness but no faithfulness. If we are being filled with the Spirit—which is another way of saying that we are under the Spirit's control—then this composite picture of Christian character will be manifested in our lives. It is the character of Jesus Christ being recreated in our lives through the work of the Holy Spirit as we are being sanctified and made more like Him.

There will be love—*agape* in Greek, the love of the will. It is not the love of emotion or physical attraction or family bond. It is the love we choose to demonstrate in self-sacrifice, the noblest kind of love. There will be joy—a deep down satisfaction that all is well. There will be peace—an inner calm that comes from knowing that God is in charge of everything. There will be longsuffering—patience that enables us to endure difficulty. There will be kindness—tender concern toward others. There will be goodness—moral and spiritual excellence. There will be faithfulness—loyalty and trustworthiness. There will be gentleness—the word really means humility or meekness. Finally, there will be self-control—the ability to restrain passions and appetites.

Wherever the Spirit of God is in control, all of these characteristics are manifest. Then Paul adds this interesting note: "Against such there is no law." Paul has been writing in Galatians about the difference between life under the law and life in the Spirit. His point here is that if you live in the Spirit you do not need an external law. An external law can never force someone to have this kind of character. Law cannot produce these traits. They flow from within by the ministry of the Holy Spirit. It is an incredible miracle that the Spirit can produce these attitudes in our lives, one that should fill our hearts with gratitude. It should make us eager to yield ourselves to the Spirit by walking in obedience to His revealed Word so that we can see this kind of character manifested in us.

MEDITATE *on* THESE THINGS

> Finally, brethren, whatever things are
> true, whatever things are noble, whatever
> things are just, whatever things are pure,
> whatever things are lovely, whatever
> things are of good report, if there is
> any virtue and if there is anything
> praiseworthy—meditate on these things.
> —*Philippians 4:8*

There goes today's newspaper! I guess we can't be reading that. So much for the television! If we took seriously this command to meditate only on what is true, noble, just, pure, lovely, of good report, virtuous, and praiseworthy, it would severely limit our reading and viewing, wouldn't it? To some extent we are all the product of what we take into our lives. You know the old computer maxim: garbage in, garbage out.

Jesus once said something profound that seems to make a contrary point. He said that it is not what goes into a man that defiles him; it is what comes out of a man that defiles him (Mark 7:15–23). The real problem is not that the world outside threatens to defile us. The real problem is what is deep inside us. It is our fallen nature, the flesh. Sin does not come from the outside in; it comes from the inside out. That is a point that the apostle Paul made over and over.

But here Paul is telling us that there are still all kinds of things outside that can excite the sin nature inside us. If you want to live a life that honors God, you cannot continue to let things into your life that are likely to draw you in the direction of disobedience. You have to make a decision to focus on what is good rather than on what is evil. You have to choose to fill your mind and heart with things that God would praise rather than things you would be ashamed to have revealed.

This is the focus you should have. Focus on what is true, not what is false. The truth encompasses all of God's revelation, known most clearly in Christ and in the Scripture. Focus on what is noble, what is worthy of your respect. Do not waste your attention on people or media you could never respect. Focus on whatever is just—what is right by God's standard. Focus on things that are morally pure and things that are lovely and pleasing. So much of what we are offered as entertainment—in our time as in Paul's—highlights immorality and ugliness; do not dwell on such things. Focus on whatever has a good reputation, whatever is virtuous and worthy of praise. Meditate on these things, and you will be cooperating with the Holy Spirit who is working to produce these traits in your life.

Your Body Is *a* Temple

> Do you not know that your body is the
> temple of the Holy Spirit who is in you,
> whom you have from God, and you are
> not your own? For you were bought at a
> price; therefore glorify God in your body
> and in your spirit, which are God's.
> —*1 Corinthians 6:19–20*

We often operate from the assumption that we own our bodies. Even if we do not own much in this world, at least we have our bodies. We assume we have a right to control them. But the Bible tells us something very different. We do not belong to ourselves. We have been bought and paid for at a very high price. The price, as we saw in chapter 4, was "the precious blood of Christ, as of a lamb without blemish and without spot" (1 Peter 1:19). Your body is a building that has been purchased and is now inhabited by its new owner. Once you were just an old house, but you have had an extreme makeover and are now a temple in which God lives. Your body is the temple of the Holy Spirit, so you are obligated to use that temple in a way that honors Him.

A friend of mine was visiting New York City with a companion and wanted to show him the grand St. Patrick's Cathedral on Fifth Avenue. It happened that the companion was a Roman Catholic, and he asked to see the shrine of his patron saint, St.

Joseph. The two of them found the niche where a statue of St. Joseph stood, but there was a sign hanging around St. Joseph's neck that said, "DO NOT WORSHIP HERE. THIS SHRINE IS OUT OF ORDER." This shrine is out of order? My friend apologized to his companion, but he said to himself, "I wonder if there aren't many days when that sign should be hanging around *my* neck. "DON'T EXPECT TO SEE CHRIST HERE. THIS SHRINE IS OUT OF ORDER."

Your body is that shrine. It is that temple to the Holy Spirit because the Holy Spirit lives there. Sometimes I'm afraid He is obscured. Sometimes His fruit is not visible in my life. Sometimes my body is filled with things that are not true, pure, and praiseworthy. Make sure your shrine is in order, that people may see your life and glorify your Father in heaven. Glorify God in your body and in your spirit, which belong to Him.

BLAMELESS *on the* DAY *of* CHRIST

That you may become blameless and harmless, children of God without fault in the midst of a crooked and perverse generation, among whom you shine as lights in the world, holding fast the word of life, so that I may rejoice in the day of Christ that I have not run in vain or labored in vain.

—*Philippians 2:15–16*

Paul's motive as he exhorts believers is that he wants to rejoice in the day of Christ. The day of Christ is the day when we all get to heaven and see Him face to face. What would make that a day of rejoicing for Paul? He is not thinking here about his joy in seeing Christ. He says that a source of joy on that day will be seeing the believers with whom he had ministered standing in the Lord's presence, seeing them rewarded because they had lived blameless and harmless lives and shined as lights in a wicked world.

Later in this letter (4:1) Paul calls the Philippian believers his joy and his crown. In 1 Thessalonians 2:19 he says that his joy and crown of rejoicing will be seeing the believers he served standing in the presence of our Lord Jesus Christ at His coming. What a wonderful perspective on ministry! It is an eternal perspective, oriented toward that future day of accountability, and not simply wanting to be judged blameless himself but wanting to see those he taught being judged blameless.

Paul did not say, "I want to have a big church. I want to have success in ministry so that people will see that I am effective." He did not care about his reputation. He had a heavenly perspective. He said, "When I get into the presence of the Lord, I want to know that my efforts had eternal consequences." That was why he wrote his letters, why he preached the gospel, why he exhorted the churches. He wanted to see changed lives, lives that would be pleasing to Christ on that day.

He wanted these children of God to live blameless, harmless lives—which means lives that were innocent, unmixed with sin. He wanted them to live without God's reproach in the midst of a crooked generation. The Greek word for "crooked" is the one from which we get "scoliosis;" it means twisted or perverted. If Paul's generation was twisted, ours certainly is as well. He wanted the believers to shine as lights in a dark world. The way you do that is to hold out the Word of life, proclaiming the gospel from the Word. He wanted his people to live like that so that they could share an eternal reward from Christ.

Don't you want to hear the Lord say, "Well done, good and faithful servant"? I do. I need to keep a heavenly perspective like Paul. I want to live my life, not for the approval of men but for the approval of the Lord Himself. I want to minister to people, not so I can enjoy their respect but so I can rejoice in their reward in Christ's presence. Today there is so little of living in the light of the day of Christ. We get caught up in pleasing people and making this life comfortable. Those things are so unimportant from an eternal perspective. We need to lose our lives in anticipation of the day when we see Jesus Christ and can rejoice over the fruit of a life lived as a shining light in the world, faithfully proclaiming the Word of life.

THE HEART OF THE BIBLE

THE HOPE *of* HIS APPEARING

> Teaching us that, denying ungodliness
> and worldly lusts, we should live soberly,
> righteously, and godly in the present age,
> looking for the blessed hope and glorious
> appearing of our great God and Savior
> Jesus Christ.
>
> —*Titus 2:12–13*

The Bible calls us to live in the light of the return of Jesus Christ. Most Christians understand that Jesus is returning. It's all through the New Testament. In recent years we have been preoccupied with a fictional approach to the Second Coming, reading the *Left Behind* series and other novels about what the future might be like when Christ returns. But it is very important that we get beyond the fictional and begin to live in the reality of the coming of Jesus Christ. It is not just a subject for curiosity. It is an event that gives direction and purpose to our lives.

We should live in anticipation of that wonderful event. We should "love His appearing," as Paul says to Timothy (2 Timothy 4:8). We should be able to exclaim with John at the end of Revelation, "Come, Lord Jesus!" (Revelation 22:20). You may ask, "Why would I look forward to that day? Why would that be a blessed hope for me? Life is wonderful here. We have love and family and children and all the wonders of the world. Why would we look forward to the end of life as we know it? Why would we want to live every day thinking about the Last Day when Christ will appear?"

Let me give you two big reasons. First, this world at its best is far, far short of what heaven is going to be. I hope you never lose sight of that. With all the joy we find in this world as Christians, the world is still a place of darkness and suffering, and we live, as we have seen, in the midst of a crooked and perverse generation. I hope you never become so attached to this world that heaven does not interest you any more. What God has prepared for us is infinitely beyond the best this life can offer. "No eye has seen, no ear has heard, no mind has conceived what God has prepared for those who love him" (1 Corinthians 2:9 NIV).

But it is not all about you. What about Jesus Christ? How long is He supposed to endure the hostility and hatred of this world? How long must He put up with the demeaning by those who think they are wise and with their constant blaspheming of His name? When I think about the coming of Christ, I ask the question the martyrs ask in Revelation 6:10, "How long, O Lord, until You judge?" How long will You endure these indignities? How long will You allow Satan to run rampant over this planet, hindering Your work? How long will Your Holy Spirit be grieved and quenched? How long will Your church be persecuted? I long for Christ to come and set things right. I long to see

Him receive the glory and honor and praise He is denied in this world. I will delight to see Jesus appear in glory as our great God and Savior.

When Henry Martyn first went as a missionary to India, he entered a Hindu temple and saw them worshiping false gods. He wrote in his diary, "I ran out of the temple with tears. I cannot endure existence if Jesus is to be so dishonored." Does it bother you at all that Jesus is so dishonored in our world? Martyn said he could not bear to live if Christ was demeaned. I cannot take any more of this dishonoring of Christ either. It makes me long for His glorious appearing, not just for my sake, but for His.

CHAPTER 8

WHAT IT MEANS
TO FOLLOW JESUS

$$\infty$$

A CHRISTIAN IS A PERSON who can say "Jesus is Lord" (Romans 10:9). Being a Christian means accepting Jesus' authority as Lord and Master. The salvation Jesus offers is indeed a free gift—not something we can earn by being good—but the gift is the right to become a Jesus-follower who is being transformed. The gift is not the right to stay as you are.

Jesus did not seek people who would believe intellectually that He was the Son of God and then go their own way. He sought people who would believe in Him—trust Him completely with their lives and submit to His authority. It makes no sense to say that Jesus is Lord and then refuse to obey Him. He said, "Why do you call Me 'Lord, Lord,' and do not do the things which I say?" (Luke 6:46). Genuine belief in Jesus includes obedience.

We'll see in this chapter that becoming a disciple of Jesus means giving up your own life and offering yourself to God completely. It means being transformed by the Word of God so that you do the will of God and do not have to be ashamed before Him. It means giving up this world's values and living by Jesus' values of lowliness and love.

DENYING YOURSELF

> Then He said to them all, "If anyone desires to come after Me, let him deny himself, and take up his cross daily, and follow Me. For whoever desires to save his life will lose it, but whoever loses his life for My sake will save it."
> —*Luke 9:23–24*

Jesus attracted huge crowds which included all kinds of people. At the center were the Twelve, the chosen ones who had left everything to follow Him, who were later known as the apostles. But there were many other disciples. The word "disciple" means learner or student, and there were people in the crowd at all stages of learning from Jesus. Then there were those who were merely curious and the thrill-seekers for whom Jesus was like the circus coming to town. They just wanted to see miracles.

Also included in the crowd were Pharisees and other religious leaders who were there only to try to catch Jesus saying something wrong so they could do away with Him.

Luke tells us that Jesus spoke to all of them. From that mixed crowd He was seeking those who would truly commit themselves to Him. As preachers do today, Jesus gave an invitation to the crowd, although it may not sound like any invitation you have heard. He said, "If anyone desires to come after Me, let him deny himself, and take up his cross daily, and follow Me." If you want to be a true disciple, you will have to pay the supreme price to follow Me. In order to gain your life, you must lose it. If you are not willing to do that, you will lose it in the end in eternal judgment.

We live in a day when the gospel has been made so easy that I fear it is not the gospel anymore. Often the invitation we give is not a legitimate invitation to follow Jesus. It is what I call "easy believism." You often hear an invitation to accept Christ, which implies that all you have to do is believe intellectually or say a few words or walk the aisle, without having to change anything about your life. We rarely hear a clear statement that to accept Christ you must deny yourself and give up any claim to your own life.

But that is what Jesus says: You must deny yourself. Becoming a Christian is the end of you as you have known yourself. It is the end of your hopes, your dreams, and your goals. It is a decision to put yourself to death—not by suicide but by turning away from your old self and finding a new identity in Christ.

Jesus even said that to follow Him you must hate your own life (Luke 14:26). When Martin Luther began the Protestant Reformation in 1517 by posting his ninety-five *theses* on the church door in Wittenberg, Germany, the fourth thesis said that if you are going to follow Christ you must engage in self-hate. That sounds very strange to us today. Most presentations of the gospel today are about self-fulfillment rather than self-denial. But Jesus is very clear about what He is after. To deny someone is to refuse to be associated with that person, as Peter later denied Jesus and refused to be associated with Him. When you come to Christ, you come because you refuse to be associated with your old self. You are sick of yourself and in desperation you willingly give up that empty life.

The commitment to Christ involves taking up your cross daily. What does that mean? It does not mean bearing the heavy burdens of life. The cross meant only one thing in the time of Jesus. It meant a painful and shameful death. Jesus was saying, "If you want to follow me, it is the end of you—not just your hopes and dreams, but maybe your physical life. But even if you literally lose your life for my sake, it will be worth the cost, because you will gain your life forever, eternally." Is that the invitation to

which you responded when you became a
Christian? Is that the way you are following Jesus?

NOT LOVING *the* WORLD

> Do not love the world or the things in the
> world. If anyone loves the world, the love
> of the Father is not in him. For all that is
> in the world—the lust of the flesh, the lust
> of the eyes, and the pride of life—is not of
> the Father but is of the world. And the
> world is passing away, and the lust of it;
> but he who does the will of God abides
> forever.
>
> —*1 John 2:15–17*

The basic command here is "Do not love the
world." What does John mean by "the world."
Clearly he does not mean the people of the world,
since John 3:16 says, "God so loved the world." Does
he mean the planet earth? Of course not. God
created this planet with all its beauty and richness,
and gives us "richly all things to enjoy" (1 Timothy
6:17). Does he mean things of beauty in this world,
things of benefit, things of comfort? No, he is not
prohibiting our enjoyment of those things.

"The world" here means the evil world system in
which we live. "The world" includes all that is
opposed to God and His kingdom. It is the invisible
spiritual system dominated by Satan, the "ruler of

this world" (John 12:31). It is the world that hates Jesus (John 7:7) and hates His followers (John 15:19). Christians are no longer "of this world" (John 17:16). If we love that old evil world, "the love of the Father" is not in us.

What is "the world" like? It is characterized by three things: "the lust of the flesh, the lust of the eyes, and the pride of life." The world is that evil system that panders to our passions, panders to our vision, and panders to our pride. The world comes at our self-centeredness. The world wants us to focus on what we want. We want to fulfill fleshly passions. We want what we can see, what we can possess for our own benefit. We want people to think we're important and better than them. That's what the world is all about.

But that is not what the Father loves, so as believers we are not to love that. We are tempted by it. Sometimes we fall into the sins of lust and pride, but when we do, we hate it. Sometimes we feel like the apostle Paul in Romans 7:15: "For what I am doing, I do not understand. For what I will to do, that I do not practice; but what I hate, that I do."

We do fall into these things, but we do not love them. They are part of the old evil world that is "passing away," whereas we are part of the new world that God is transforming. We are not under the power of the Evil One, but under the authority of the Father.

We are those who are motivated and character-ized by doing the will of God. Therefore we will abide forever—we will live eternally. It is not because we do the will of God that we will live eternally, but because we belong to Him and have received eternal life that is manifest in our obedience to Him.

BEING TRANSFORMED

> I beseech you therefore, brethren, by the mercies of God, that you present your bodies a living sacrifice, holy, acceptable to God, which is your reasonable service. And do not be conformed to this world, but be transformed by the renewing of your mind, that you may prove what is that good and acceptable and perfect will of God.
>
> —*Romans 12:1–2*

It will help you understand these verses if you start at the end and work backwards. The goal of these commands is "that you may prove what is that good and acceptable and perfect will of God." In other words, the point is to live a life that is pleasing to God, in the center of His will.

How do you do that? By being "transformed by the renewing of your mind." This principle is found all through Scripture. Transformation occurs as the

Holy Spirit changes our thinking, as we meditate on God's Word. As the Word takes root in your heart, it shapes your thinking, and your mind is made new. I am fortunate to be able to spend so much time in the Word of God in my calling as teacher and preacher. My mind is renewed every week of my life, and that bears fruit in biblical thinking. It is a transforming experience to let the Word of Christ dwell in me richly (Colossians 3:16). If you want to live a life that is in the center of God's will, a life that is acceptable to Him, then you need to allow your mind to be renewed continually by the transforming power of biblical truth.

This involves not letting yourself be conformed to this world. Here "the world" is not the same word we saw in 1 John. Here it is literally "the age," the eon. It refers to the spirit of this age. Do not let yourself be pushed to think and act the way this present age does. Don't let the culture dictate your thinking and your values. The first century had its pagan and secular ways of thinking and acting, just as the twenty-first century does. Paul says that as Christians we must not allow ourselves to be shaped by the world's thoughts and behaviors.

The key to all of this is to present our bodies to God—not just our physical bodies, but our whole selves. We are to offer ourselves as living sacrifices, giving up our lives. As we have seen, this is what Jesus demands when He tells us to deny ourselves and take up our cross. We give up our claim to our bodies and our lives. We die in order to live.

We are used to thinking of sacrifices in the Old Testament as dead. Animals were killed before they were placed on the altar and burned. Those sacrifices had to be holy and acceptable to God and were an act of worship. Paul says that you should think of yourself like that kind of sacrifice. Get up on the altar and offer yourself to God. It is often said that the problem with living sacrifices is that they keep crawling off the altar. You have to decide to be a living sacrifice who chooses to remain on the altar, not just killing yourself once for all but every day choosing not to live for yourself but for God. This, Paul says, is "your reasonable service," or more literally, your logical worship.

Do you want to be in the will of God? Let your mind be transformed by being renewed by the truth of God's Word. Avoid being conformed to this world. Get up on the altar and sacrifice yourself as an offering to God. I beseech you to do that. Based on what? Based on all "the mercies of God" which are yours in Christ. He has been so good to you. It is only reasonable to offer yourself back to Him.

LOVING ONE ANOTHER

> A new commandment I give to you, that
> you love one another; as I have loved you,
> that you also love one another. By this all
> will know that you are My disciples, if you
> have love for one another.
>
> —*John 13:34–35*

Jesus says that the mark of true Christianity is love within the fellowship of believers. The commandment to love was not new. Jesus Himself pointed out the two greatest commandments of the Old Testament, the command to love God (Deuteronomy 6:5) and to love your neighbor (Leviticus 19:18). But Jesus' command to love is new in two respects. First, the love within the disciples is different from the kind of love we demonstrate to all neighbors in need. Second, Jesus said that we are to love "as I have loved you." He is giving us a new model for this kind of love.

What is the model? It is what Jesus did just before He gave the new commandment. In John 13, the disciples had gathered for the Passover meal in the Upper Room. Jesus knew that later that night He would be betrayed and arrested, but John says that "having loved His own who were in the world, He loved them to the end" (John 13:1). Knowing that it would be their last time together before the Cross, Jesus showed them how to love one another.

In the ancient world, people got their feet dirty because they wore sandals on dusty roads. Formal meals like the Passover lasted a long time, and the participants reclined on the floor around a low table, so that your neighbor's feet were not far from your head. It was a common courtesy to provide a servant who would wash the feet of the guests. It was a menial job for the very lowest of servants.

The disciples had gathered with Jesus for the supper, but there was no one to wash feet. They had been arguing about which of them was the greatest, so none of them wanted to do anything to diminish his status. No one would stoop to do foot-washing. But Jesus did. He got up from the table, wrapped a towel around His waist, took a bowl, and washed the filthy feet of His selfish disciples. They were stunned and embarrassed. Peter said, "No, Lord, you cannot wash my feet," but Jesus did it anyway. It was a demonstration of His lowliness and the humble love that stoops to do whatever is needed.

It was a wonderful gesture, but it did not come close to the demonstration of lowliness that came when the One who was equal with God went all the way to the Cross to bear the wrath of God for our sins. Paul says in Philippians 2:6–8 that when Christ humbled Himself to become one of us, He did not come halfway down and appear to us as a king. When Christ came down from heaven's glory, He came all the way down. He made Himself of no reputation. He humbled Himself and became a servant. He went all the way down to the lowest point of human experience, a shameful death on a cross.

That is how Jesus loved us. So when He said His new command was to love one another the way He loved us, that's what He meant. The model for love is humbling ourselves to do the most menial task to meet another person's need. Even beyond that, the model for love is sacrificing ourselves for another, giving our lives for one another. If you live like this, Jesus says, the world will know that you are followers of Me.

RIGHTLY DIVIDING *the* WORD

> Be diligent to present yourself approved to God, a worker who does not need to be ashamed, rightly dividing the word of truth.
>
> —*2 Timothy 2:15*

Do you want to be "approved to God"? Do you want God to be pleased with your life? I'm sure you want to please the One Who loves you, Who gave His Son for you, Who will bless you in this life and someday welcome you into His presence. It is part of being a Christian to want to please God.

But how do you present yourself to God for approval? You have to be "a worker who does not need to be ashamed." Have you ever been ashamed of your work? I remember a project in wood shop in junior high school. We had to make a lamp, but my lamp was really lousy. The wood was not cut very well or sanded well. The lamp did not work well. As I recall, the teacher came by and said, "John, you ought to be ashamed of that. You can do better." I was a worker who needed to be ashamed.

No doubt you have had times when you have been ashamed of the quality of your work. You blew a play in a big game. You didn't read the recipe carefully for an important dinner. You failed to study for a test. You mowed the yard so sloppily that the grass stood up between rows and around the edges. The Scripture is saying to us that if we want to be approved to God, we need to be workers who take our work seriously and give it our best effort, so that we will not have to be ashamed when we stand before God.

What is the key to being a worker for God who does not need to be ashamed? The key is "rightly dividing the word of truth." If I want God to approve my work, I must rightly divide all of Scripture. What does "rightly dividing" mean? Literally, it means to cut it straight like a carpenter cutting wood straight so that furniture fits together, or a mason cutting stone straight so that pieces of a wall fit together perfectly. Paul was a leather worker who had cut hides into neat pieces that he could sew together to make a tent. Rightly dividing was all about precision and accuracy. He is telling Timothy to handle the Word of God with precision and accuracy, to interpret and apply it correctly.

If you want to live a life that warrants God's approval rather than shame, then you must handle the Word of God rightly. Interpret it in the light of God's love and righteousness revealed in the Cross. Do not soften its demands or its promises. Allow it to transform your heart, so that your mind is renewed. Then you will know what it is to live in the center of God's will.

CHAPTER 9

BRINGING LIGHT *to the* WORLD

$$\infty$$

B‌EING A DISCIPLE OF JESUS CHRIST can never be reduced to merely producing Christian character in ourselves or loving one another, as important as those things are. Being a disciple of Jesus means making other disciples, because that is what our Lord has commanded us to do. God's sovereign purpose in this world is to create a redeemed people to worship and enjoy Him eternally, but He has chosen to accomplish that purpose through human beings. He has made us stewards of the gospel, placing that precious knowledge in earthen vessels, in the fragile container of our lives.

I assume that you are reading this book because you are a Christian, and you understand that sharing the good news of eternal life through faith in Christ is every Christian's responsibility. You may know that and still not tell anyone about Jesus. Do you think you do not know enough to be an evangelist? Do you think you need more training? I doubt that is your problem. In the unlikely event that you knew absolutely nothing about the Bible before you began reading this book, by this point you know enough to tell someone how to become a Christian. You could take the verses on the Cross and salvation in chapters 4 and 5 and lead someone to Christ.

The problem for most Christians is not knowledge but obedience. It is not that we do not know what we need to do or how to do it. What we lack is the intention to do it. We have not made up our minds that the commands of Jesus will come before the demands of this world. When we genuinely deny ourselves and follow Him, when we offer our lives as living sacrifices, our minds and hearts will be transformed. As disciples of Jesus, our first priority will be to make other disciples for Him.

Why *the* Church Is Here

Go therefore and make disciples of all the nations, baptizing them in the name of the Father and of the Son and of the Holy Spirit, teaching them to observe all things that I have commanded you; and lo, I am with you always, even to the end of the age. Amen.

—*Matthew 28:19–20*

Do you ever wonder what our real purpose is in the world? Here is the end of your confusion. Our purpose is to make disciples of all the nations. The risen Jesus Christ gave this command to His apostles just before He ascended to the Father, but He intended it for all of us. That is why these verses are known as the Great Commission. It states the mission of the church.

In the original Greek, there is only one verb here—"make disciples." That is the imperative. The other words that seem like commands are actually participles modifying the main verb. What I mean is that the main verb in the sentence is "make disciples," which you do by going, baptizing, and teaching (all participles).

To make disciples in another nation, you have to go where people do not know about Christ. Once you get there and they come to faith in Christ, you have to baptize them in the name of the Father and of the Son and of the Holy Spirit. That is to say, you need to bring them to an understanding of God as Father, Son, and Holy Spirit, which is demonstrated in baptism. Baptism is important not because it saves, but because it is the public confession of salvation. Then you instruct them to be obedient to their Lord, teaching them to obey everything Jesus commanded. You are not alone in this enterprise. Jesus says, "I am with you always, even to the end of the age." Until the time is completely done for evangelism, I will be with you helping you to make disciples.

How would you answer if I asked you the reason for the church? Why are we still here on earth? What should we be doing?

Some might say we should be living a holy life. That is a good thing, but it is not the main reason we are here. If that is all the Lord wants, we might as well go on to heaven, because we can't really live a perfectly holy life down here.

Some might say we are saved so we can be in fellowship. That is good, too, and we do have fellowship with other believers. But the fellowship is very imperfect, as you must know from experience. We have all kinds of problems getting along with one another as Christians. We don't actually do fellowship very well down here.

Some might say the real priority for us is worship. We do work on worship in the church, but we don't always get that right, either. Sometimes our minds wander and we find it hard to focus on God. Sometimes our emotions are swept away by music, but they go to a place that has little to do with God. We are fickle creatures, easily distracted.

All of that is to say that our holiness is imperfect, our fellowship is imperfect, and our worship is imperfect. If those were the top priorities, then we would do better to go on to heaven. When we get to heaven, we will be perfectly holy; our fellowship and worship will be perfect. That leaves us with only one reason to stay here on earth. There is one thing we can do on earth that we cannot do in heaven—that is to make disciples of all nations. The Great Commission is given to us individually and corporately as the church.

Make sure you are involved in carrying out this commission. No one is exempt from this joyous duty. Go to people who do not know Christ. Tell them about the Father, the Son, and the Holy Spirit. Encourage them to acknowledge faith in Jesus Christ and to demonstrate that by baptism. Follow up by teaching them to obey the things Jesus told us to do. And do it all knowing that Christ Himself is with you as you accomplish His purpose for you. He will be with you to the very end.

THIS LITTLE LIGHT *of* MINE

Let your light so shine before men, that they may see your good works and glorify your Father in heaven.
—*Matthew 5:16*

This may be one of the first verses you learned in Sunday school. No doubt you sang the song: *This little light of mine, I'm gonna let it shine.* Jesus said that we (His disciples) are the light of the world. We must not hide that light under a bushel or in a church building. We must let it shine. How will people see that light? Through our good works.

The German atheist philosopher Nietzsche once said that if he saw more redeemed people he might be more inclined to believe in their Redeemer. Christians who do not have changed lives have a credibility gap. If I am trying to tell you how great my doctor is, but I am dying under his care, you might question his skill. If I try to tell you how great my auto mechanic is, but my car is belching black smoke out the exhaust, you will probably be reluctant to entrust your own vehicle to him. What good does it do to tell people how great our Savior is if they cannot see that we ourselves have been saved from sin? Let your light shine.

What does Jesus mean by light? Jesus also calls Himself "the light of the world." John calls Him "the life that is the light of men," "the light that shines in the darkness" (John 1:4–5) The light in us is His light, the indwelling Christ, the Holy Spirit within us. The apostle Paul speaks of "the light of the gospel of the glory of Christ" (2 Corinthians 4:4). We have that light shining through our lives if our actions reflect the nature of Christ—His love, compassion, and forgiveness. His light shines through our attitudes, words, and deeds. When people see that our lives have been changed so that we have Jesus' values and see the power of God at work in us, they will agree that we do have a great Savior. When they see redeemed people, they are more inclined to believe that we have a Redeemer. The Christlike life is the platform on which individual testimony becomes convincing.

The alternative is for the Christian to live in the dark. Scripture teaches that "God is light and in Him is no darkness at all. If we say that we have fellowship with Him, and walk in darkness, we lie and do not practice the truth" (1 John 1:5–6). If no light shines from your life, either you have no relationship with Christ or you are bringing dishonor to Him. It is a sad thing for someone to proclaim Jesus Christ as Lord and Savior and continue to live an openly sinful life. It brings disrepute to Christ and the gospel. It is a stumbling block for unbelievers. It is certainly not effective in convincing anyone that Christ has the power to transform lives. Our responsibility as disciples and evangelists is to have lives so transformed by the Word and the inward presence of Christ that everyone can see His light reflected in our acts of kindness.

PRAISE *as a* FORM *of* EVANGELISM

I waited patiently for the LORD;
And He inclined to me,
And heard my cry.
He also brought me up out of a horrible pit,
Out of the miry clay,
And set my feet upon a rock,

And established my steps.
He has put a new song in my mouth—
Praise to our God;
Many will see it and fear,
And will trust in the LORD.

—Psalm 40:1–3

In the recovery of an emphasis on the value of praise in recent years, we have relearned what the psalmist knew—that praise has an evangelistic impact. Worship is ultimately the goal of evangelism. Our goal is to help more and more people enjoy God and glorify Him forever, to share God's work of gathering for Himself a people from every nation, tribe, and tongue, who will worship Him in heaven. But worship is also a means of evangelism. I do not believe that the lost person or seeker is capable of worshiping and coming into the presence of a holy God. But that lost person can see and hear us praising God and be brought to faith in Him. The psalmist says that when I have a new song of praise in my mouth, many will see it and be awestruck by our great God and come to trust in Him.

A believer filled with praise makes a tremendous impact on a sinner. We have a new song, the song of the redeemed, and it produces hope in a despairing heart. The psalmist says, "I was in a horrible pit. I was stuck in miry clay. I was hopeless and helpless, but the Lord heard my cry and lifted me up. He set my feet on a rock and gave me a solid place to

THE HEART OF THE BIBLE

stand." That is a picture of salvation. God in His grace stoops down to pick a sinner up out of the pit and sets him on a new, safe path. The response to that amazing unilateral act of mercy is a new song—a song of praise, a song of redemption.

The more we sing that song, and the louder we sing it, the more people will hear it. Those who are still in the pit, stuck in miry clay, will see how we were lifted out by God's love and see hope for themselves. Be filled with praise every day, because God not only is worthy of our praise but also may use your praise to draw people to Christ. Your song may lead them to open their hearts to the Savior, so that they might see Him perform His great rescue in their lives as well.

CHAPTER 10

OUR ETERNAL DESTINY

THE GOAL OF THE CHRISTIAN LIFE is not a holy life or a useful life. The goal is to be with God in heaven, completely transformed into the likeness of Christ, enjoying God's presence fulltime, "lost in wonder, love, and praise." That is our ultimate destiny and the destination of our pilgrimage through this life. Paul says, "Our citizenship is in heaven" (Philippians 3:20). We are like those people of faith in the Letter to the Hebrews who are "strangers and pilgrims on the earth" who seek a homeland, a heavenly country (Hebrews 11:13–16). Peter begins his first epistle by referring to believers as strangers or pilgrims. We are not home yet. We are just passing through.

It is rare today for Christians to live in the light of that hope. The old hymns show that there was a time, not so long ago, when both death and heaven were more real to us. In today's America of relative wealth and comfort, with the progress of medicine and the cultural denial of the reality of death, we think less of heaven than believers in other countries and other times. We need to recover our sense of heaven as our true home. We need to remember, in good times and bad, that this world is not all there is. We need to remind ourselves, as Paul says, that "For the things which are seen are temporary, but the things which are not seen are eternal" (2 Corinthians 4:18).

OUR HOPE *and* OUR INHERITANCE

> Blessed be the God and Father of our Lord Jesus Christ, who according to His abundant mercy has begotten us again to a living hope through the resurrection of Jesus Christ from the dead, to an inheritance incorruptible and undefiled and that does not fade away, reserved in heaven for you.
>
> —*1 Peter 1:3–4*

There is a lot of theology packed in these verses, which start by saying, "Blessed be God." Which God? The only true God, the God and Father of our Lord Jesus Christ. He is the same God who is called the God of Abraham, Isaac, and Jacob in the Old

Testament. He is the One called Almighty, Lord of Hosts, Maker of heaven and earth. In the New Testament He is the Father of Jesus Christ. That means He shares the same eternal life, the same essential nature as Christ. You cannot be acknowledging the true God unless you are acknowledging the God who is also the Father of Jesus Christ, who is one with Him. The God revealed in the incarnate Lord Jesus "has begotten us again to a living hope."

What is that hope? It is the hope of eternal life, that we too will be raised from the dead to be with Christ in heaven. We have that hope because we know that God raised Jesus from the dead. Jesus said, "Because I live, you will live also" (John 14:19). He also said, "He who believes in Me, though he may die, he shall live" (John 11:25). We live this life in the midst of God's blessings here and now, but with the constant hope that we will one day share the joy of resurrected life with Him.

We have a treasure waiting for us. It is our inheritance as children of God and joint heirs with Christ (Romans 8:17). It is "an inheritance, incorruptible," one that will never come to an end, one that will never decay or be defiled. It will never fade away like the things of this world. It is being preserved for us, as Jesus said, "where neither moth nor rust destroys and where thieves do not break in and steal" (Matthew 6:20). Our real treasure is in heaven, not in this world, which is passing away. The reward awaiting us in heaven is eternal life, life without corruption, life without defilement, a glory that will never fade.

As we live our Christian lives, we not only enjoy what God has done for us in giving us a new birth, we not only enjoy the abundant blessings and mercies He pours out upon us, but we also enjoy the hope of eternal life. We have our hope fixed on the day when we receive the inheritance reserved for us in heaven.

WE SHALL BE LIKE HIM

Beloved, now we are children of God; and it has not yet been revealed what we shall be, but we know that when He is revealed, we shall be like Him, for we shall see Him as He is. And everyone who has this hope in Him purifies himself, just as He is pure.
—1 John 3:2–3

"We are children of God." Right now, if you believe in Jesus Christ and have been redeemed and justified, you are a child of God. But "it has not yet been revealed what we shall be." Someday you will be changed, and the fact that you are a child of God will be evident to everyone, because you will be transformed into the likeness of Christ. Just seeing Christ in all His glory will have the power to transform us.

But in this present world, we have not yet

experienced what Paul calls "the revealing of the sons of God" (Romans 8:19). To some degree our status as God's children remains hidden to the world and to us. It is true that people can see God's light reflected in us to some degree by our good deeds, and Christ's nature ought to be seen in the fruit of the Spirit in our lives. Nevertheless, you can't just look at someone walking by and know if that person is a child of God or not. Someday that will all change.

When Christ is revealed—at the Second Coming when Christ is seen not as the humble suffering Servant but as the Lord of all, coming in power and glory—we will see Him as He truly is. Until then we see Him only through a glass darkly, or a dim reflection in a poor mirror, but then we shall see Him face to face (1 Corinthians 13:12). The whole world will see Him when He arrives as the powerful, shining figure we see in the Book of Revelation, riding a white horse.

There is coming a day when the whole world is going to find out who we really are. We ourselves will only then discover who we really are. Your real life, your true self, is now hidden with Christ in God. "When Christ who is our life appears, then you also will appear with Him in glory" (Colossians 3:4). What a thought! We are going to be like Christ, because we will see Him as He is.

What difference does it make that we live with this hope? "Everyone who has this hope in Him purifies himself, just as He [Christ] is pure." If you live in anticipation of Christ's coming, it changes the way you live. When I was in elementary school, I was a serious discipline problem. The teacher would not let me do all the things I wanted to do, so whenever she left the classroom I went wild. Once I was jumping from desk to desk just as I heard her orthopedic wedgies come through the door, and I was caught in mid-flight. If I had anticipated her coming, I would have altered my behavior.

We know that Christ could come at any time. We know that He is perfectly pure and holy. When He comes, we want Him to find us living pure lives. We don't want Him to catch us doing whatever we please because we think He will never return. Jesus told stories about tenants who thought the landlord would never return. But our Lord is coming back and He will call us to account. The good news is Christ will not only come as Judge but as Savior. Not only will He reveal our impurity, but in His mercy He will reveal our eternal nature as children of God, and make us pure "as He is pure."

TRANSFORMED *into* HIS IMAGE

> But we all, with unveiled face, beholding as in a mirror the glory of the Lord, are being transformed into the same image from glory to glory, just as by the Spirit of the Lord.
>
> —2 Corinthians 3:18

Someday we will see Christ face to face and be changed by His glory, but this verse says that even in this life we are being transformed by seeing His glory. This verse says that unlike Moses or the prophets or the saints of the Old Testament, believers are able to see God's glory in an "unveiled way," more clearly than people in the past ever could.

Moses saw God's glory, but only partially, seeing God's "back side." The people of Israel saw God's glory as a glowing at a distance. Moses had to wear a veil over his face so that people would not see God's glory directly and be harmed—and, Paul suggests, to keep them from seeing that the glory in his face was fading away. But now the glory of God has been revealed clearly in the face of Jesus Christ. John says, "We beheld His glory, the glory as of the only begotten of the Father, full of grace and truth" (John 1:18). Paul says a few verses after our text that we have "the light of the knowledge of the glory of God in the face of Jesus Christ" (2 Corinthians 4:6).

When I say "glory," I mean all the attributes of God. They are revealed to us in the Old Testament, but they are revealed most clearly in the living person of Jesus. The glory—the revelation of God's true nature—shines more wonderfully in Christ than in any other place. So here we are with the veil off, looking directly into God's glory and all His attributes revealed in Christ. That vision, that knowledge, is transforming us into His image, from one level of glory to the next, as the Holy Spirit works in our lives.

This verse is not telling us about a future glorification but about present sanctification. If you gaze at the glory of God revealed in the face of Jesus Christ as presented in the New Testament, it will change you. It is the Spirit that works that transformation as Jesus Christ becomes our consuming vision and we become increasingly like Him.

A PLACE PREPARED *for* US

> In My Father's house are many mansions;
> if it were not so, I would have told you. I
> go to prepare a place for you. And if I go
> and prepare a place for you, I will come
> again and receive you to Myself; that
> where I am, there you may be also.
> —*John 14:2–3*

On Jesus' last night with His disciples before He went to the Cross, He gave them many wonderful promises. But none was more wonderful than the promise that begins His farewell discourse. It was the promise that He was leaving them for the purpose of preparing a place for them in heaven with His Father, and that He would come back to take them there.

These are familiar and comforting words, but the idea of a house with many mansions inside it does not make much sense. What Jesus meant in the original language was "In My Father's house are many rooms." When I was a child, I used to think of heaven as a whole bunch of mansions. I heard preachers ask, "How close is your mansion going to be to the throne?" They talked as if you might be within walking distance, or you might be way out on the edge of town. One preacher even said that your mansion would be made of the materials you ship up there—whether wood, hay, and straw, or gold, silver, and precious stone. (That was not Paul's point in 1 Corinthians 3:12!) Unfortunately these pictures of heaven as a neighborhood of three little pigs' houses of brick or straw get stuck in our minds.

That is not what Jesus is saying. There is only one house—the Father's—and it has many rooms. I'm not living 15 blocks away or on the wrong side of the tracks from His house; I'm living in it, and so are you. We will be together with the Lord and live forever with His people as one family in one house.

What is the Lord Jesus doing right now? He is in heaven, getting ready to welcome His brothers and sisters, His adopted fellow heirs. He is waiting for the day when He will come to take us all home to be with Him. That is the event we call the Rapture, when Jesus comes and snatches away His redeemed people from this evil world. He will bring the church, all true believers, to heaven, where we will have a huge celebration the Book of Revelation calls the marriage supper of the Lamb. We will dwell in the house of the Lord forever, enjoying the Father's house throughout eternity, enjoying all the things God has prepared for those who love Him.

Your Labor Is Not *in* Vain

> Therefore, my beloved brethren, be steadfast, immovable, always abounding in the work of the Lord, knowing that your labor is not in vain in the Lord.
> —*1 Corinthians 15:58*

In this country, we labor for rewards. There is nothing improper about working for pay, and the Bible sees nothing wrong with promising rewards for those who trust God and live for Him. Very few people want to work for no reward. That was why the communist economy eventually collapsed. I was in a hospital in Kiev, Ukraine, just after the Soviet Union had fallen apart. I met a cardiac surgeon and went into the woefully inadequate operating room. I asked how it was to be a surgeon under communism. He replied, "We don't have any equipment and we don't get paid much." I asked how much. "Fifteen dollars a month." That was hard to believe. As I was leaving the hospital I saw a woman sweeping the steps with a broom she had made from twigs. I asked someone how much she made. The answer: "Fifteen dollars a month."

Everyone got the same reward. That was the communist notion of justice. It did not provide much motivation to become a surgeon.

The Lord promises that our labor for Him will not be in vain or unrewarded. There are rewards that all believers will share. This verse comes at the end of a discussion of the resurrection we will share with Christ, when we will all be given new spiritual bodies and death will be defeated forever. We know that we will all share the reward of being in our Father's house in heaven, and we will all gather around His throne in praise.

But we will each have to give account for our work. We will have to answer whether the hope of salvation made us complacent or whether it made us "steadfast, immovable, always abounding in the work of the Lord." Jesus tells us that "your Father who sees in secret will Himself reward you openly" (Matthew 6:4). He promised, "The Son of Man will come in the glory of His Father with His angels, and then He will reward each according to his works" (Matthew 16:27). Paul wrote that "each one will receive his own reward according to his own labor" (1 Corinthians 3:8). In the last chapter of the Bible, Christ says, "Behold, I am coming quickly, and My

reward is with Me, to give to every one according to his work" (Revelation 22:12).

The reward may not be prosperity in this life or public acknowledgement in this world, but when we stand before Christ everything we did for Him will matter. Every act of mercy, every sacrifice, every witness for Him will count. None of it will be in vain. He is keeping a record of your faithfulness, and in His grace He will reward you on that day when you see Him face to face.

SUBJECT INDEX

SCRIPTURE INDEX

*This verse or passage is discussed by the author, beginning on the page cited.

THE MACARTHUR
SCRIPTURE MEMORY SYSTEM

JOHN MACARTHUR POURS HIS HEART into his work as a Bible teacher, and now he teaches Scripture, literally one verse at a time, with The MacArthur Scripture Memory System. The System comes in a turned-edge book, complete with the following timeless elements:

- 3 audio CD's with Dr. MacArthur reading the verse-of-the-week, and providing a brief statement of what that verse means and why it is so important to remember.

- A handy pack of printed cards, one for each verse, so that you can put one in your wallet or purse to refresh your memory of the weekly verse.

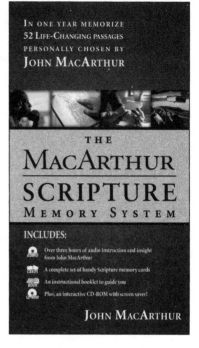

IN ONE YEAR MEMORIZE
52 LIFE-CHANGING PASSAGES
PERSONALLY CHOSEN BY
JOHN MACARTHUR

THE
MACARTHUR
SCRIPTURE
MEMORY SYSTEM

INCLUDES:

Over three hours of audio instruction and insight from John MacArthur

A complete set of handy Scripture memory cards

An instructional booklet to guide you

Plus, an interactive CD-ROM with screen saver!

JOHN MACARTHUR

ISBN: 0-7852-5061-1

- CD-ROM containing a dynamic desktop complete with the text of week's verse and a link to listen to the audio of the verse! Also contains a screen saver with each week's verse.

For old and new Bible readers alike, The MacArthur Scripture Memory System is an excellent way to really get into the Word and commit it to memory.

NELSON REFERENCE & ELECTRONIC
A Division of Thomas Nelson Publishers
Since 1798
www.thomasnelson.com

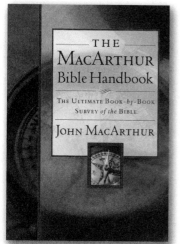